Scripts and Sketches

Edited by John O'Connor

Heinemann is an imprint of Pearson
Education Limited, a company incorporated in England
and Wales, having its registered office at Edinburgh Gate, Harlow,
Essex, CM20 2JE. Registered company number: 872828

Heinemann is a registered trademark of Pearson Education Limited

10

ISBN 978 0 435233 30 3

Cover design by Miller Craig & Cocking
Cover photography by Stone
Typeset by ⌐\Tek-Art, Croydon, Surrey
Printed in China (CTPS/10)

Contents

Introduction

Scripts and Sketches is a completely new collection of short plays for use in the Key Stage 3 English and Drama classrooms. Produced by experienced leading writers such as Gene Kemp and Farrukh Dhondy, the scripts introduce students to a wide variety of genres, from social realism to comic parody.

Issues covered range from the influence of video games to our attitudes to old age, and high-quality material is provided for the exploration of questions concerning social responsibility and citizenship.

Each script is accompanied by activities consistent with the aims of the Literacy Framework, which will help to develop students' skills in speaking, reading, writing and drama.

I hope that students will be challenged, intrigued and entertained by these new scripts, and that the resource as a whole will be a welcome addition for the busy classroom teacher.

John O'Connor

Say Yes!

Steven Deproost

List of Characters

Laura
Loudspeaker
Q
Gabrielle
Chorus
Matt

LAURA	(*thinking and breathing heavily with nausea*) Oh my head! I feel sick. Where am I? What's going on? I must sit up. Oww! (*She vomits.*) Eurghh. There's a glass of water by the bed. (*She drinks.*) That's better. But the smell is awful. Must get some help.
	(*Out loud. First call rather soft and phlegmy.*) Hello?
	(*Clears her throat.*) Hello?! Is anybody there?
	(*Silence. She sighs. Whirr of an electric motor. Thinks.*) What's that? A camera. (*aloud*) Hello! I'm here, I'm awake! (*thinking*) I'm wearing a gown. So where are my clothes? Is this a hospital? Perhaps if I open the door. Up we get. Easy does it. That's not so bad. (*She tries the door.*) Locked. Locked? Why? Just a minute. How did I get here? I was going somewhere . . . with Matt . . . then an ambulance . . . (*aloud*) Matt! Matt! (*She rattles the door handle.*) Let me out!
LOUDSPEAKER	Move away from the door, please.
LAURA	Who's that?
LOUDSPEAKER	Go back to the bed, please.
LAURA	Where are you?

LOUDSPEAKER	There's a speaker in the wall. Now get into the bed, please, and someone will come in. That's right.
LAURA	I've been sick.
LOUDSPEAKER	Don't worry, everything's under control. Lie down, please. Thank you.

The door is unlocked and opened. Q enters.

Q	Hello, Laura.
LAURA	Hello.
Q	Don't get up. It's best to lie down for the time being. Take it easy. We're just removing your little mishap. (*noise of sucking/cleaning machine*) That's better. I think you'll find the atmosphere more pleasingly fragrant. Nothing like the smell of freshly exuded vomit to make you vomit all over again. How are you feeling now?
LAURA	Are you a doctor?
Q	I am here to make you better.
LAURA	Are you a doctor?
Q	I have thoroughly examined your condition and reached a diagnosis. And with your co-operation we can proceed to a successful treatment with full remission of your symptoms.
LAURA	But there wasn't anything wrong with me – not till this . . .
Q	Ah, Laura. So often people with life-threatening conditions ignore the symptoms which stare them in the face.
LAURA	What symptoms?
Q	They go into denial.
LAURA	I haven't got anything to deny!

Q	I rest my case.
LAURA	Can you stop playing games with me and tell me what's going on? What's happened to Matt?
Q	He is being taken care of.
LAURA	What are you doing to him? I want to see him now. (*She gets up and starts to hit Q.*) Let me out of here. I want to go home . . .
Q	Calm down.
LAURA	You've no right to keep me here.
LOUDSPEAKER	Do you require assistance, sir?
LAURA	Let go!
Q	(*to speaker*) No, we're getting on just fine. Aren't we, Laura? You can send Gabrielle up.
LAURA	Let go! Let go! Let go! (*She cries.*)
Q	Now sit down again. We're going to look after you. Here, have a tissue. You'll feel better soon – once you've had the treatment.
LAURA	(*still tearful*) I don't need any treatment.
Q	If you co-operate, when we've finished you can see Matt again. How about that?
	Laura sniffs.
Q	I'll take that as a 'yes' then. (*knock at the door*) Ah, just on cue. Come in! (*Gabrielle enters.*) She's all yours. (*to Laura*) Laura, this is Gabrielle: she's going to begin your treatment. If you're a good girl, you'll be out in three or four days. (*to Gabrielle*) I think you'll find her reasonably tractable. (*leaving*) If you run into trouble, just give me a call. I'll be with the other one.
GABRIELLE	Will do, sir. Now then, Laura, are you going to say hello? (*silence*) Don't be shy. The quicker we get

	started, the quicker you can leave – and the quicker you can see Matt again.
LAURA	Is he all right?
GABRIELLE	Look at me and say hello.
LAURA	Hello.
GABRIELLE	Well done, Laura. Good start. OK. There are three phases to your treatment – the three Rs. Recognition. Re-education. Re-integration. These will become clear as we go along. So let's begin with Recognition. Why do you think we've brought you here?
LAURA	I don't know.
GABRIELLE	Really? I find that hard to believe. When was the last time you went to school, Laura?
LAURA	I don't know.
GABRIELLE	When was the last time you did any on-line shopping?
LAURA	I don't know.
GABRIELLE	When was the last time you accessed the Internet? – No, let me guess . . . you don't know. Perhaps if you went to school you'd know a bit more. Let's try a little harder, shall we? Or we could be here for a long time. Do you possess a mobile phone?
LAURA	Yes.
GABRIELLE	Correct. Cool. We're on our way. Have you used it?
LAURA	No.
GABRIELLE	Correct again. Now we're cooking! I've got a few things in this bag that I'd like you to identify . . .
LAURA	My clothes!

GABRIELLE	So you admit that these are your garments? The jacket, the trousers, the T-shirt, the knickers, the scarf, the socks – odd, and the booty things.
LAURA	Yes, of course. Can I put them on?
GABRIELLE	No. But I would like you to examine them. Is there anything strange about them?
LAURA	I don't think so. They're a bit faded.
GABRIELLE	Yes, and . . . ?
LAURA	Unfashionable.
GABRIELLE	Definitely, and . . . What's missing from all of them?
LAURA	What do you mean?
GABRIELLE	None of them has a . . . ?
LAURA	I don't know.
GABRIELLE	Oh come on, don't start that again.
LAURA	I don't know.
GABRIELLE	I think you need to try a little harder.
LAURA	(*in tears*) I don't know.
GABRIELLE	I think you do really.
LAURA	You know the answer already.
GABRIELLE	But I want to hear it from you. Not one of these items has a . . . ?
LAURA	(*with difficulty*) Label.
GABRIELLE	At last! Good girl. No labels, no logos, no brand names. And that's not all. We know that you read old paper books in preference to the free on-line editions with banner and marginal advertising. Furthermore you have been observed with Matthew in the woods on several occasions, deliberately engaging in entertainment of no commercial value.

LAURA	That's not a crime is it, even under this government?
GABRIELLE	As you were taught in Primary School, Laura, we were born to consume. The wheels of industry and the clicking of dot commerce depend on it. Without consumption our whole economy would collapse. Branding, marketing and advertising are essential to our well-being and it is the duty of every citizen to be open to them. You have wilfully ignored that duty like someone who puts her fingers in her ears when her neighbour cries out for help. But you're right. That is not a crime. The government respects the rights of the individual.
LAURA	So, why am I here?
GABRIELLE	You were also found in possession of these – which cannot by any stretch of the imagination be merely for individual consumption. Do you deny it?
LAURA	How can I?
GABRIELLE	Five hundred Class A leaflets inciting people to join you in your madness.
LAURA	What about free speech?
GABRIELLE	Your group is getting too big. We have a duty to protect the innocent.
LAURA	What do you want me to do?
GABRIELLE	It's not a question of what I want you to do – it's what you must do for yourself and the rest of society.
LAURA	What do you want me to do?
GABRIELLE	I hear you. Don't worry. We just want you to be a happy member of society.
LAURA	I was happy.
GABRIELLE	We're just going to help you . . .

LAURA	What's that for?
GABRIELLE	It's nothing. Just a little jab to help you relax and make your brain more receptive.
LAURA	Oww!
GABRIELLE	Keep still. There. Nothing to it. Time for the Re-education Room . . .
CHORUS	(*Spoken or sung as jingles. Experiment with echoes and different acoustics. Sense of time being compressed*)

Welcome. Welcome to the Re-education Room.
The place where life begins
again . . . and again . . . and again . . .
Shopping, shopping, shopping, shopping
Shopping's so much fun!

Shopping, shopping, shopping, shopping
Fun for everyone!

New, Unique, Exciting, Sexy, Designer

Choice, choice, choice, choice, choice, choice, choice, choice, choice . . .

Bored with your house?
Bored with your spouse?
Bored with who you are?
Don't just sit there, have a make-over –
Endless varieties of self
Straight off the shelf.
Make a resolution to buy the solution.

Sayesco [*SAY-YES-CO*] for all your needs
The one-stop store with more, more, more.

Hardware, software, homes and lifestyle.
Food, fashion, fun and family value.

Four for the price of three.
Three for the price of two.
Two for the price of one.

Buy two get the second at half price.

Buy one get one free.

Buy one of *these* and get one of *those* for 20p.

Buy a hundred and get a discount on one of our
exclusive package holiday deals.

Shop at Sayesco, double the value, half the price –
That's nice!

Double points on Thursdays!

Triple points if you spend over £50.

Vouchers for your schools.

Can't face preparing food?

For meals in a moment to stay or to go

Come on down to Sayesco.

The Sayesco Deli: gourmet gratification in every
slice –
That's nice!

Shop at Sayesco for life with a little extra spice –
That's nice!

Come to our restaurant for special curry and rice –
That's nice!

Too tired to stray from your sofa?

That's me.

Want to stay at home?

Yes, please!

Then shop on-line at www.sayesco.com and order
in a trice –
That's nice!

Sayesco, Sayesco, Sayesco, Sayesco, Sayesco,
Sayesco, Sayesco –
That's nice!

Q   Now then, Laura, I bet that didn't seem like three
days, did it?

LAURA	No.
GABRIELLE	Retail Therapy is so rewarding.
LAURA	Yes.
Q	You look great in your new clothes.
GABRIELLE	Very cool.
Q	And now the time has come for Re-integration.
GABRIELLE	Time to go back home.
LAURA	Can I?
Q	Of course. This isn't a prison.
GABRIELLE	Don't forget your mobile.
Q	And here's a book of vouchers with our compliments.
LAURA	Thank you.
Q	It's a pleasure.
Q AND GABRIELLE	Have a good life.
	Outside.
LAURA	Matt!
MATT	Laura! (*They hug.*) Are you OK?
LAURA	Course I am.
MATT	They didn't get you on their side, then?
LAURA	You must be joking. They're not that clever.
MATT	As if they could influence our thoughts!
LAURA	Let's celebrate.
MATT	Let's go and find some decent food. I'm starving.
LAURA	What do you fancy?
MATT	How about special curry and rice?
LAURA	Mmm. That's nice.

Get 'Em

Farrukh Dhondy

List of Characters

Hem
Kay
Oss
May

NOTES

1   The stage is an open space divided into half by an imaginary
    line. One half is a dingy hotel room with a bed, a table, a sink
    with a mirror and a phone next to the bed. One wall of the
    hotel room has a rectangular frame large enough for two
    figures to perform within it. It is the imaginary Video Monitor
    screen.

2   The characters in the play can be male or female and their
    names in the play allow this flexibility. They are referred to as
    'he' but the reader must switch to 'she' as appropriate. The set
    can be realistic or consist of simple suggestive props. Only the
    frame must be represented.

3   Our action is set somewhere in Britain in the early 2000s.

*One half of the stage, the hotel room, is lit. The other is in darkness.
Hem is in the hotel room. He is at a basin and has his sleeve rolled
up and is washing a wound on his lower arm. Then he goes to a bed
and tears a sheet and takes a long piece of the sheet and ties it, as
best he can with one arm, round the wound. He looks at it. Then he
sits in the chair. He is bored. He picks up an imaginary phone.*

HEM   Reception? (*He looks at the phone. He waits. Finally there's an
      answer.*) Hello, reception? Yeah. Room 651. How do I
      switch on the video? Yes, I'm not sleepy, OK? . . . Pound
      coins in the slot? Where's the slot? Right. Thanks. Good

night. Sleep tight. You're not sleeping? On duty . . . You took your time answering. Good night for later, then, miss.

Hem gets up and finds the slot for the coins, digs in his pocket and puts in a pound coin. He throws an imaginary switch and the other half of the stage lights up. Hem drags his chair to face the imaginary dividing line of the stage. He is staring into the other half of the stage and from opposite sides of that half two characters approach carrying a chair each. They are Kay and Oss. They place the chairs to face Hem and sit on them and fold their arms.

Hem picks up the phone again.

Reception? Where's the instructions? For the game? Yes . . . I've put the money in. You don't know? I don't know either. I've wasted a pound? What a cheek. Hey, careful! What do you mean? What do you mean where have I been? None of your business. Oh you mean have I been on this planet? Look, I don't need any lip from you, miss. I'm paying for this room. (*He bangs the phone down.*) What a cheek.

There's a knock at the door.

What?

MAY   Me!

Hem recognises the voice and cautiously opens the door. He holds his wounded and bleeding arm.

May comes in. He is wearing a coat and out of the pocket he pulls a revolver and tries to hand it to Hem.

You dropped something.

HEM   Yeah. (*He takes the gun and throws it on the bed.*) I can't call a doctor to the hotel room, they'll get suspicious.

May looks at the wound.

MAY	You're not about to die. J will get here in a few hours if it's clear. He'll get you patched up.
HEM	Where's the packet?
MAY	J's got it.
HEM	I thought you were bringing it. I want to get out of here.

May picks up the interactive remote control of the TV game. He presses a button.

KAY	Hi, I'm Kay. Welcome to 'Get 'Em', the fully interactive video game.
MAY	Yeah, right! If it was fully interactive, you could hear me.
KAY	I can.

May looks at Hem.

MAY	What's this? (*a little laugh.*)
HEM	What do you mean?
MAY	I mean the damn thing is talking to me.
OSS	Never seen an interactive game before? Don't waste your money, my friends, the meter will run out. What shall we play?
MAY	What's normal? What do other people play?

Oss looks at Kay.

KAY	We give them a situation, like a war or a car chase, or a race in space against the ace, that sort of thing. We ask them to put us in a story. They make up a story.
HEM	What sort of story?
KAY	Any story. Like three guys do a robbery at an auction house and it goes wrong and one guy gets shot. The alarm goes off. They escape in different directions . . . That sort of thing.

May and Hem look at each other. It has to be a coincidence.

And you can choose your weapons.

HEM   What weapons?

OSS   Anything you like. Bows and arrows, guns, machine guns, ray guns, rockets, zappers, flame throwers, missiles, sticks and stones, name it, you can have it.

May takes his coat off and we see that he is wearing a shoulder holster with a revolver. He takes it off and puts it on the bed.

MAY   Guns make me itch. I'll have rockets, grenades and a couple of bombs.

OSS   You got 'em. Now choose a situation. Put us somewhere. Space station? Mountainous country? Auction house? Pirate ship? And then we've got to have something you want to get from us. Like a map, or the secret of the universe or just a packet of diamonds.

MAY   A packet of diamonds, eh? OK, I'll take that. And the place? Lock you geezers up. Away, inside. You're in a jail, banged up and without any weapons – just a blunt nail file.

KAY   That's fine, but then when you blast us, you won't be able to find the diamonds, they'll be blown to smithereens. And it's not very sporting, is it? Your game.

MAY   Didn't ask you, did I?

OSS   It's a waste of your time too. We don't have a chance. One grenade and we can't move, we're dead.

MAY   Yeah and I win.

OSS   Sure, but is that the point?

MAY   That's always the point. In a war, get the bigger stick.

KAY   What about giving us a secret weapon?

MAY   No!

KAY   But maybe the game allows us to have one. You know what I'm talking about, don't you, Hem?

HEM   What do you mean?

KAY   You didn't expect the little girl who opened the safe at the auction house to have a gun in there, did you? You could be dead. Thank your stars she was trained to shoot for your arm.

May and Hem look at each other. May goes round the back of the symbolic telly, making a circuit of the stage.

MAY   What the hell is going on here? Who are these guys?

HEM   Yeah, what's the game?

OSS   We told you. The game is what you make it, but it's always called 'Get 'Em' – which can mean anything. Interactive. Right?

Hem and May are puzzled.

KAY   OK, we're locked up. See bars all around us. Now at the top of the screen you have your choice of weapons. Reach for them. Grenades, bombs and flame throwers, you said?

May presses his remote control.

MAY   Right, hand over the diamonds or I'll blast you to hell.

Kay now holds up his hand and reaches for a secret weapon. From the air, as if by magic a funny 'space' gun descends and he grabs it.

KAY   You got to think again. The game allows me a secret weapon. See? An X-gun which can find you anywhere in the world and turn you to dust. It can also dissolve iron bars.

MAY   Talk about sporting! Doesn't give me much of a chance.

As he speaks we see that Hem has got hold of the revolver from the holster, checked it for bullets and crept round the back of May. He holds the gun to May's head.

HEM   Right first time.

May puts his hands up.

MAY   What are you doing, Hem?

HEM   Take a guess.

MAY   Everyone in the hotel will hear the gun shot. Don't be a
       fool.

KAY   He's right. Take him out of town and shoot him on the
       motorway and dump his body. Like he did to J.

HEM   What?

OSS   Sorry. Wasn't that part of the game? He didn't come here
       to wait . . . with you . . . for J. He's got rid of J. He came
       here to blow you away.

HEM   You . . . ! Where are the rocks?

KAY   He's got them. But he's hidden them.

MAY   Don't be a fool. You don't believe these guys. They're not
       real. They're cartoons – a damned video game . . . J's going
       to turn up . . . They're lying . . . It's only a game . . .

*While he talks Oss has left his part of the stage and reappears at
the door through which May came in. There is a violent kick to the
door. The lock gives way and Oss comes in with a revolver. He
holds it to Hem's head while Hem holds a gun to May's head.*

OSS   Drop it.

Hem drops the gun.

       I *have* got a silencer. And you too – keep your hands up.
       Now tell me, where are the diamonds you took this
       morning from the auction house? Go on. I can do
       without them, after all I'm only a cartoon, right? But
       you'll be dead.

MAY   Buried. My aunt's back garden, one foot to the right of the
       drain.

OSS   Where? Address!

MAY London. 37 Tollingford Gardens.

OSS Did you get that, Kay? Hey, hey. Whooop! No more getting bombed and shot. We can get out of here. We're rich!

Kay steps through the screen. He holds a machine gun and he shoots the three others down ruthlessly. They die.

KAY You mean I'm rich.

He picks up the phone.

Reception? My money's run out on the video. I haven't finished my game . . .

The whole stage fades to dark. Sounds of computer game zapping and shooting and bombing.

The Mobile

Mark Morris

List of Characters

Baz
Daz
Gaz

A classroom at break-time. The room is empty. The door slowly opens and Baz's head peers in, looking around. His head is quite low down. Another head, Daz's, appears above the first. A third head, Gaz's, appears above the other two. Convinced that the room is empty, Baz starts to straighten up.

BAZ   Come on, there's no one . . .

Before he can finish, he bumps into the others, who are looking over the top of him. They all stumble into the room noisily and end up in a heap on the floor.

(*to Daz*) Ssshhhhhh!

DAZ   (*to Gaz*) Ssshhhhhh!

GAZ   (*looking around, then to no one in particular*) Ssshhhhhh!

BAZ   (*whispering*) Will you pair belt up! If we get caught in 'ere we're in big trouble.

DAZ   (*to Gaz*) Yeah, belt up, will you!

The three boys get to their feet and quietly close the door behind them.

GAZ   What we doin' in 'ere, Baz?

BAZ   Lookin' for a phone, you twonk! Now shut up.

Baz and Daz begin searching the room. Gaz scratches his head and looks puzzled.

GAZ	There's a phone at the end of Clayton Street, Baz. It's bust too, you don't have to put any money in.
DAZ	(*slowly shaking his head*) Not that sort of phone. A mobile phone.
GAZ	I got one 'ere.

Gaz begins to reach inside his jacket.

BAZ	No, you sad geek. We're looking for a mobile phone to nick.
GAZ	Oh. Right.

They continue searching. Gaz still looks confused.

	Baz?
BAZ	What?
GAZ	What sort of phone are we after? There's lots of different sorts y'know.
BAZ	I know that. I want a Z-R-T-50.
DAZ	What? They cost a fortune. My dad wanted one for work but said they cost too much. They're amazing things.
GAZ	What's a Z-R-wotsit do, then?
DAZ	Can it send messages?
BAZ	Course it can. And pictures.
DAZ	Internet?
BAZ	Anything you want. Instant access.
DAZ	How many hours' standby?
BAZ	You don't have to charge it. It's got an everlasting battery.
DAZ	Has it got one of those organiser things?
BAZ	Yep.
DAZ	And answer service?
BAZ	Yep.

DAZ	Calculator?
BAZ	Yep.
DAZ	Touch-tone memory?
BAZ	Yep.
DAZ	What about games?
BAZ	Hundreds. All the new stuff.
DAZ	How many tunes has it got?
BAZ	As many as you want. You can record them. And it plays mini-discs.
DAZ	(*sarcastically*) I suppose you can watch the telly, too?
BAZ	Actually, you can, but you need a special chip to get all the digital satellite channels.
GAZ	How do we know there's one of these phone thingies in 'ere, then?
DAZ	Coz Jez sez, that's how.
GAZ	Jez sez?
DAZ	Yeah, Jez sez. Jez sez Kaz was in a lesson in 'ere, and she told 'im it got confiscated.
GAZ	(*to Baz*) What duz Daz want with a phone that was constipated?
BAZ	Look, Gaz, I'm going to say this very slowly. Snot-bag Smith took a phone off a kid in this room. The phone is really flash, Kaz sez, so we're gonna nick it. Then we're gonna sell it to Des. Then we go on the raz.
GAZ	What's the raz, Baz?
BAZ	The raz! The razzle! Buy some beer, you know!
GAZ	Oh, the raz, I see. Soz, Baz.
BAZ	Good, now shut up and keep looking. Sooner we do the biz, sooner we're out.
GAZ	Do the what?

BAZ	The biz! The business you moron!
GAZ	Oh . . . I get it . . . Do the biz, go on the raz! (*to himself*) Do the biz, go on the raz, do the biz, go on the raz . . .

Baz sighs. They keep searching for the phone.

	Hey, Daz!
DAZ	What?
GAZ	Kaz is my cousin.
DAZ	So what?
GAZ	Duz Baz know Kaz is my cuz?
DAZ	No. Duz cuz matter?
GAZ	It might. Des sez he hates Kaz coz Kaz is my cuz and he might not buy the phone.
DAZ	Good point. Hey, Baz.
BAZ	What?
DAZ	Gaz and Kaz.
BAZ	What about Gaz and Kaz?
DAZ	(*pointing to Gaz*) She's his cuz. Gaz sez Des hates Kaz. If she's his cuz and Des sees Gaz, no raz!
BAZ	I haven't a clue what you're talking about.
GAZ	It's simple, Baz. Des hates me. And so he hates Kaz coz Kaz is my cuz. He might not buy the phone coz of me and Kaz. Soz, Baz!
BAZ	So why duz Des hate you?
GAZ	Hassle with the fuzz.
BAZ	What hassle?
GAZ	Hassle with fuzz on a buz.
BAZ	Fuzz on a buz?
GAZ	Yeah, fuzz on a buz. He got thrown off and blamed it on me.

BAZ   Rozzers chucked him off a buz? What's that got to do with uz and that phone?

DAZ   What duz buz mean? I'll tell you. (*pause*) Ready?

BAZ   I think so.

DAZ   Right. Des hates Gaz coz of fuzz on a buz.

BAZ   Got you.

DAZ   Well . . . if Des hates Gaz he hates Kaz too, coz Kaz is Gaz's cuz.

BAZ   (*uncertainly*) Right . . .

DAZ   So he might not buy the phone. Soz, Baz, but them fuzz on a buz means it don't matter if we duz the biz.

GAZ   No raz, Baz?

BAZ   Doesn't look like it now . . . We'll just have to say the phone's nothing to do with Gaz and Kaz.

DAZ   Or fuzz on a buz.

BAZ   Them as well. We'll just tell him we nicked it. Won't even mention Gaz and Kaz. Then he'll do the biz and we go on the raz, Daz.

DAZ   Brilliant.

BAZ   Sorted.

GAZ   Great. I'm burstin' for a waz, Baz. Let's get this phone and go.

Baz sighs and shakes his head. They all continue to search the classroom.

Windfalls

Steven Deproost

List of Characters

Flora
Max Sails

> *The end of a garden. To one side a back gate. Centre stage an apple tree loaded with ripe apples. Windfalls around the tree. Two empty baskets. Flora enters from another part of the garden carrying a stepladder and wearing a baby-sling over her coat. She is about seventy-five years old. She puts the ladder up under the tree, climbs and begins to pick apples which she places in the sling. She registers, but ignores, a distant doorbell which is rung several times with increasing insistence. She continues to pick apples. Max Sails enters cautiously through the gate. He is in his twenties, dressed in suit and tie and carries a clipboard. He does not spot Flora. He surveys the garden. Flora watches him from the ladder.*

FLORA Can I help you?

MAX Mrs Bramley?

FLORA Yes.

MAX Pleased to meet you at last. Max Sails.

> *He offers her his hand. She uses it to get down off the ladder.*

Don't fall.

FLORA I won't. If you've got a good grip. (*Once down, she empties the apples from sling to basket before going back up the ladder.*)

MAX I rang the bell several times, but nobody answered. So I came round. To have a look.

FLORA No law against looking.

MAX   No. (*Silence. Then, of the garden*) It's big. Must be a full-time job looking after all this. It's more than I could manage. Hard work.

FLORA   You get used to it.

MAX   Can't be getting any easier for you.

FLORA   Put the windfalls in the other basket while you're standing there. It's getting dark.

Max is encumbered by his clipboard and throws the apples with one hand.

Don't throw them! – they've got enough bruises already.

MAX   Sorry. (*He tries to deal with the clipboard and continues to pick apples.*) I know the old-style nursing homes often had a bad press. But 'Resthaven' means no need to worry about laundry or cooking or cleaning. Haircare, foot care, visiting opticians and hearing-aid specialists – it's all taken care of. Splendid gardens to sit and enjoy without any of the effort of digging and weeding. Every room has its own en-suite toilet and TV point. You can have a telephone installed at normal BT rates and everyone can bring three items of their own furniture with them. (*He pauses but gets no response.*) The restaurant and day lounges are very comfortable – the whole place is centrally heated of course. And there's a full programme of craft activities, entertainment and coach outings. It's just like being on holiday. Permanently. 'Resthaven' will be a real benefit to the community – a secure place for residents to make the most of their sunset years. (*Pleased with this flourish, he bites into an apple.*) Urghh!

FLORA   They're cookers.

MAX   You won't be able to cope for much longer. Taking thirty feet off the end of this garden makes a lot of sense.

Acorn Developments will pay you instead of you having to pay for a gardener. It's the last piece of the jigsaw. We get access into Chestnut Lane, the community gets a fabulous facility and you're sitting on a small fortune. What do you think?

FLORA   You've missed some. You'll have to speed up a bit. It's getting darker.

He obeys her for a while, then . . .

MAX   Look. Never mind the bloody apples. We're talking a two million pound project here with £80,000 for you and first pick of a room. (*no response*) £100,000 maybe. You're an old woman. You can't read the letters I send you. You can't hear the doorbell. I know all the changes in the last twenty years must be confusing, but you seem to have totally lost touch with the modern world. (*A phone rings. Max reaches for his mobile.*) Max Sails here.

But the phone continues to ring. Flora extracts one from her clothing.

FLORA   Hello, love. Yes, I'm just finishing. Yes. You bring the video, I'll get something out of the freezer. OK. (*She comes down and stuffs apples in Max's pockets.*) Thank you. At the end of the day a bit of help can make all the difference.

She walks off towards the house leaving Max to find his clipboard and the way out in the rapidly gathering gloom.

The Bully

Gene Kemp

List of Characters

Jim the narrator
Jim (at school)
Dave (Jim's friend)
Mum (Jim's mother)
Houseman's gang (three)
Houseman
Mr Tomkins (Jim's teacher)

SCENE **1**

Outside bus stop.

JIM THE NARRATOR It was just a normal day of the week for me, or so I thought when I woke up at the usual time to go to my job as an office junior. It was the same as I waited at the bus stop until I woke from my daydreaming and looked across and saw someone I hadn't seen for about five years, someone who had given me hell in my first year at secondary school and whom I certainly didn't ever want to see again.

It brought back that old, old feeling of terror which the sight of him and his friends had aroused in me all that time ago. His name was Houseman. This morning, years later, he wasn't looking my way and hadn't seen me.

I tried to think about the day at work ahead, that gorgeous new girl in the office, the motorbike I was saving for – anything – but I couldn't stop my mind drifting back to the first year at secondary school, an all-boys school unfortunately. Now I wish I'd gone to a Co-Ed.

The years rolled back. I was twelve, little, weedy, scared, fresh from primary school.

Jim and Dave outside in playground in large secondary school.

DAVE   Do you know where we gotta go for our next class?

JIM   Search me. This place is massive, innit? Makes our old school look mini.

DAVE   What d'you reckon to this place, then?

JIM   I like it so far, I think. What about you?

DAVE   Yeah, it's OK. Pity there's no girls here, though, but you can't have everything, I suppose.

JIM   Most of our class seem all right. No bigheads or anything.

DAVE   How come you was late this morning? I thought we were going to catch the bus together.

JIM   I missed it and got lost in the main building on the other side of the bridge.

DAVE   *(laughs)* You berk. You're not supposed to go over that side.

JIM   Well, I didn't know. I've only been here three days, remember.

DAVE   Look, there's some kids from our class over there. Let's follow them. They might know where to go.

JIM   OK.

SCENE 3

Home at weekend. Home is comfortable but not plushy.

MUM   How was your first week at school, then, Jim?

JIM	Fine. Quite exciting, really. Loads to see and do. Not a boring moment. Still finding my way around the place.
MUM	Oh, good. You know, I was a bit worried about you going to such a big school. You're quite happy, then?
JIM	Yeah. My old mate Dave's in my class and the other kids are OK. Our form teacher Mr Tomkins, he's all right as well.
MUM	That's a load off my mind, then. Hey, your bag weighs a ton. You haven't got too much homework, I hope?
JIM	No, Mum. It's no problem. I can handle it.
MUM	I hope you'll be happy there, then, cos since your Dad left, you know I couldn't afford to send you anywhere else really.
JIM	I don't want to go anywhere else, Mum. I'm quite happy there. It's great.

SCENE 4

Walking up the hill to school with Dave. Some older pupils waiting outside sitting on the wall. One of them, wearing school uniform, but with DMs and trousers too short for him and a skinhead haircut, approaches Jim.

BOY	What's your name?
	He shoves Jim, who stumbles back.
DAVE	Leave him alone.
	Two other older boys shove him away, leaving Jim with the first one.
JIM	Why do you want to know?

BOY	Cos I do. You better tell me.
OTHER BOY	Don't let him give you any cheek, Houseman.
JIM	Jim Sutton.
HOUSEMAN	Well, Jim Sutton, have you got any money for me?
JIM	No, I spent it on bus fare.
HOUSEMAN	I hope you ain't lying to me. (*He reaches inside Jim's blazer pocket and lifts out his dinner money.*) What's this then?

He suddenly kicks Jim viciously in the groin. Jim bends over in agony. Two of the other boys then kick Jim as well. Houseman raps him on the head with his knuckles.

Be seeing you around, Jim Sutton.

He walks away with his friends, grinning. Jim stands there, bruised, sore, near to tears.

DAVE	You OK? Sorry I couldn't help. Two of them grabbed me.
JIM	Did they do anything to you?
DAVE	Nah. Didn't seem interested in me.
JIM	That's cos you're big. No one gives you a hard time. They nicked my dinner money.
DAVE	I can lend you some if you want. I've got enough.
JIM	Thanks a million. Hey, do you know who they were?
DAVE	I think they're fifth formers. A couple of other kids have been picked on by them. Right scary crowd they are.
JIM	Well, I'm gonna keep out of their way. Trouble is, to get to our bit of the school we have to go past theirs.

DAVE	Yeah, I know.
JIM	I got an idea. There's an early bus. I'll get to school before they do. Just for a while.
DAVE	I dunno about that. I don't want to get to school too early.
JIM	Yeah, but they're not after you, are they? I can always do some homework to use up the time.

SCENE 5

Jim is playing football outside with Dave and classmates when Houseman and his gang suddenly appear.

HOUSEMAN	What's going on here, then? You ain't allowed to play football on the grass, you know.
JIM	Oh, no. What's he doing here?
DAVE	They ain't supposed to be over this side of the school.
JIM	Try telling them that.

Other classmates vanish as Houseman's gang surround Jim and Dave. Houseman grabs Jim's football.

HOUSEMAN	Oh, it's you, Jim Sutton. Haven't seen you for a while. You got any more money for me? You better have or you'll be in trouble.
JIM	No, I haven't!

They search him but don't find any this time. Houseman curses and smacks him viciously. His head spins.

HOUSEMAN	Well, I'll have this nice new football instead.
JIM	You can't take that! My mum bought it for me.
GANG MEMBER	Oh, dear. Did Mummy buy you a nice new football, then?

ANOTHER ONE	Well, Mummy's going to be cross with you now.
ANOTHER ONE	She'll give you a smacked bottom.
HOUSEMAN	We're having it now. Let's go to the toilets. I need to have a fag.

They walk away bouncing the ball. Jim rubs his aching head.

DAVE	Rotten pigs. I hate them.
JIM	Not as much as I do. Do you think I ought to tell Tomkins about them?
DAVE	Dunno. Might make things worse. They'll take it out on you afterwards.
JIM	Everyone'll think I'm a sneak, I s'pose. Well, I'm gonna watch out for 'em from now on. I won't let them get me.

SCENE 6

Standing near bus stop in a crowd.

DAVE	Nearly holiday time. What you getting for Christmas, then?
JIM	New bike, I hope. I had to walk home twice last week cos they were hanging round the bus stop. Flipping long way it was as well.
DAVE	They don't seem to be hanging around today. I can't see 'em anywhere.

A hand taps Jim on the shoulder and he looks round. Whack! A fist punches him in the mouth, splitting his lip. Dazed and feeling sick, he sees Houseman walking away with his mates rubbing his fist and grinning.

Jim is silent, bleeding – in pain.

| DAVE | What a bastard! |

JIM	(*dabbing mouth*) I feel like I've been kicked by a mule. He's got one hell of a punch on him.
DAVE	He's really got it in for you, hasn't he?
JIM	Well, if I get my new bike I'm riding to school next term. No more hanging round bus stops for me. No way.
DAVE	You gonna tell your mum?
JIM	No, I'll say I did it playing football. Don't want to worry her.

SCENE 7

Home at Christmas. Tree with new racing bike in front of it.

JIM	Gosh! Thanks, Mum. A racing bike. Just what I wanted. Fantastic!
MUM	That's all right, Jim. You've been a good lad and you've worked hard. You deserve it.
JIM	Can't wait to ride it to school. Now I won't have to catch the bus any more.
MUM	Why? What's wrong with catching the bus?
JIM	Er . . . nuthin'. Save some money on the bus fare.
MUM	Oh, yes. I hadn't thought of that. Good idea!

SCENE 8

Riding home from school next term, Jim sees Houseman's gang up ahead of him.

GANG MEMBER	Look who it is.
HOUSEMAN	Shove him off the bike.

Jim pedals faster, trying to race past them. Houseman lashes out, catching him on the side of the head. Jim falls off the bike on to the pavement banging his knees. The bike goes flying.

GANG MEMBER	He's not very good at it, is he?
HOUSEMAN	He won't be riding that for a while.

They start kicking the bike, ripping off the chain, wheels and pedals, then they walk away laughing. Dave comes along and finds Jim howling and trying to fix the busted bike.

DAVE	What happened to you? Fall off your bike?
JIM	(*Pause. Sobs before he speaks.*) Shoved off, more like. Guess who? Houseman and his thugs. I thought I was OK going to school like this. Now what?
DAVE	You gonna tell your mum this time?
JIM	Nah, don't think so.
DAVE	Why not?
JIM	No point, really. It won't be long before that lot leave school and they won't be around any more. Don't want to upset her.
DAVE	She will be when she sees that bike.

SCENE 9

Back at home.

MUM	Oh, Jim. You're late. I was worried about you. Are you OK?
JIM	Yes, Mum. I fell off my bike and grazed my knee, that's all.
MUM	You've only had that bike for a month or so as well.
JIM	I'm afraid it's going to have to be repaired. Got a bit damaged.

Mum sees the bike for the first time.

MUM (*indignant*) Jim, I wish you'd take better care! I'm hard up, you know. That bike cost a lot of money. Goodness knows how much it's going to cost to get it mended. I'm not sure I can trust you to ride it again.

JIM Sorry, Mum.

MUM Your tea's ready for you on the table. I'm going out!

Later.

MUM Is everything all right, Jim? You seem to be having quite a few accidents lately. Falling off bikes, cutting your lip, things like that. Sorry I grumbled so much. I wondered if . . .

JIM My luck's out at the moment, Mum. That's all.

SCENE 10

Walking home down the hill with Dave to catch the bus, Jim's on the alert looking out for the Houseman gang, but they come out of an alleyway and surprise him.

HOUSEMAN Get him.

Jim sprints away trying to escape. One of the gang knocks his bag out of his hands. He doesn't have time to pick it up. He hides round the corner from the bus stop. Dave arrives carrying the bag.

DAVE I'm afraid they got to your bag before I did. Take a look. I picked all of 'em up but they're all trashed.

Jim looks inside. They've ripped up all of his school books. He stifles sobs, then straightens up.

JIM That does it. I won't, I won't, I *won't* stand for it any more. I'm gonna stop them.

DAVE	What'll you do?
JIM	Tell Mum for a start. There was nearly a year's work in there.

SCENE 11

Back home.

MUM	Oh, Jim, why didn't you tell me before?
JIM	I didn't want to worry you, Mum. I thought they might stop.
MUM	Well, they didn't, did they? And now you've got a whole year's work to do again.
JIM	I'll have to copy all that stuff out again. What a drag!
MUM	They're not going to get away with this. I'll see to it. We'll get it sorted. I'm off to see your Headteacher!

SCENE 12

Nearly empty classroom on second floor at lunch-time. Jim's busy copying out schoolwork. Houseman and gang march in. Houseman comes over to Jim. He looks really mad.

HOUSEMAN	You've had it. You grassed on me, you little sneak. Got me chucked out.

He starts hitting Jim, who gets to his feet, hands covering his head and tries to run, but Houseman's mates grab him, lifting Jim off his feet.

GANG MEMBER	What shall we do to 'im, then? Give 'im a good kicking?
HOUSEMAN	No! Let's chuck him out the window.

Jim struggles furiously. As they open the window and try to lift him out he hears the door open.

| JIM | Help! Save me! Help! |

The door shuts again. They swing him out of the window, holding his legs. He sees the ground spinning around a long way down below and closes his eyes.

| GANG MEMBER | You'd better not drop 'im. It'll mean Borstal for us. |
| HOUSEMAN | I don't care. I want to kill 'im. |

The door opens again. Mr Tomkins appears with Dave and some classmates. Houseman drops Jim back in the classroom and rushes away. Mr Tomkins helps Jim up.

| MR TOMKINS | Are you all right? |

Jim splutters, unable to reply.

| MR TOMKINS | You sure you're all right? |
| JIM | (*stammering*) I thought . . . he was going . . . I . . . thought . . . he . . . was . . . going . . . to . . . kill . . . me . . . |

SCENE 13

Bus stop in first scene.

| JIM THE NARRATOR | That was the last time I'd seen him until today. The last years at school were better after he'd gone. |

As I stared at Houseman in the bus queue he turned and looked at me. I tensed, wondering if he'd do anything, but he didn't seem to recognise me. His eyes were glazed over and he looked rather depressed and lifeless. Perhaps he was on drugs or something. He looked scruffy, a bit like a down-and-out.

He'd forgotten me, but I would never forget him. Never.

Witness

Paul Francis

List of Characters

Mum (Mrs Colton)
Marie
Ben
Terry
Clare
Ms Richards

SCENE 1

Mum busy, Marie leafing through magazine.

MUM	Is everything all right, Marie?
MARIE	How d'you mean?
MUM	You and Terry. You don't seem yourself this week.
MARIE	No, I'm a bit fed up. Don't know why, really.
MUM	Is it Terry?
MARIE	Sort of. I don't know why I go out with him, really . . .
MUM	He's OK. They seem a nice enough crowd. Smart, good manners . . .
MARIE	That's for you, Mum. They're not usually like that.
MUM	I'm sure. We all have our moments.
MARIE	They can be nasty. Terry's quite racist.
MUM	Really? But he's always been charming . . .
MARIE	He knows what you're like, so he hides it when you're around.
MUM	Does he push you around, then?
MARIE	Nothing heavy, but he likes to get his own way. Shouts and stamps a bit if I want to do something else.

MUM	So, you're not seeing him?
MARIE	Not tonight. I'll see. I wonder what he's doing . . .

SCENE 2

Street corner, at night. Ben waiting impatiently. Terry arrives, late.

BEN	Terry, what took you so long? Women trouble, right?
TERRY	Watch it. Me and my women are off limits.
BEN	Yeah, Terry, sure. Where we going, then?
TERRY	Hollywood's, Bethnal Green.
BEN	The disco? Valentine's night?
TERRY	That's right.
BEN	We picking someone up, then?
TERRY	Yeah. A load of mates. And then we'll pick up someone else.
BEN	Anyone special? That Mukhta?
TERRY	Might be. Interested?
BEN	Yeah, I'm in.
TERRY	Right. Let's go.

SCENE 3

Next day, in the street.

CLARE	You didn't fancy it, then? The disco?
MARIE	Not really. Any good?
CLARE	Yeah, it was OK. Did you hear about after? This Asian lad got beaten up. I mean, really bad.
MARIE	How do you know?
CLARE	Ben was there, he told me. Hey, there's Terry.
MARIE	Was he in it, too?
CLARE	I don't know. Ask him. You still talking?

MARIE	Sort of. Well, yeah.
CLARE	(*as Terry approaches*) I'll see you, then. (**She goes.**)
TERRY	Hi. Where you been?
MARIE	Same as usual. Hanging around. What about you?
TERRY	Magic. Not hanging around at all. Did you hear?
MARIE	Hear what?
TERRY	The action. Bethnal Green, last night.
MARIE	Go on.
TERRY	We did this lad. Mukhta something. He's in hospital now. Won't be walking too good.
MARIE	What did he do?
TERRY	Not a lot. Curled up. Cried a bit.
MARIE	I mean, what did he do to you?
TERRY	Nothing. What could he do? There's one of him, and there's six of us.

Marie starts to walk away.

Marie! Where you going?

MARIE	Got to get back. I told my mum.
TERRY	Oh, sure. Good lady, your mum. Send her my love.
MARIE	Yeah. (**She turns, and walks off.**)

SCENE 4

School playground, break-time.

MS RICHARDS	Clare?
CLARE	Yes, miss? (**She comes over.**)
MS RICHARDS	Is Marie all right?
CLARE	I think so, miss.
MS RICHARDS	She's not in school. Do you know why?
CLARE	No, miss.

MS RICHARDS	I'm not trying to make trouble. I want to help her.
CLARE	Yeah, well, she'll need something.
MS RICHARDS	What does that mean?

Clare looks round, to check that no one is listening. She drops her voice.

CLARE	You know that boy who was attacked at Hollywood's?
MS RICHARDS	I saw it on the news. Was Marie involved?
CLARE	She might be, miss. Sort of.
MS RICHARDS	She is either involved or she isn't. There's no 'sort of' about it.
CLARE	Oh, she didn't do it, miss. She'd never. Her mum'd kill her.
MS RICHARDS	But if she didn't do it –
CLARE	She knows who did. She's going to be a witness.

SCENE 5

Marie and her mum, at home, have just finished their tea.

MUM	So, what are you going to do?
MARIE	I'm going to help them, Mum. They need witnesses.
MUM	But you weren't there.
MARIE	No, but I've talked to Terry.
MUM	And?
MARIE	He did it, Mum. He said so. He bragged about it.
MUM	Marie, you have thought about this?
MARIE	I'm not stupid.
MUM	No, I know. But you're special, and you know what people are like round here. If Terry's mates know you shopped him –

MARIE	Shopped him, Mum? I'm not a crook.
MUM	I know that. Sorry.
MARIE	It was you brought me up this way. You went bananas every time someone made a racist crack, gave Asians a rough time.
MUM	Yes, I know.
MARIE	So I'm doing the right thing, yeah? Well, aren't I?
MUM	I don't know, love. I hope so. Just take care, OK?

SCENE 6

Terry, hanging around in a car park. Marie approaches him.

TERRY	I thought you'd gone off me.
MARIE	Did I say that?
TERRY	No. But you showed it, sort of. I know what it is.
MARIE	Tell me.
TERRY	I'm a hero. Valentine night. The action, yeah?
MARIE	That turns girls on, does it?
TERRY	Well, you're here. The big boot does the talking, right? Well, trainer. These Reeboks. Look. (*Points at his foot.*)
MARIE	It's a dirty trainer. So?
TERRY	That bit where the laces are. That's dried blood.
MARIE	Terry –
TERRY	I'll never wash 'em, never clean 'em. That's the proof that I was there. I did my share, the night Mukhta got done. I was kicking with the best. You thought I was a wimp –
MARIE	I never said that.
TERRY	No? Whatever. Nobody's calling me a wimp now. Me, Ben, Jason . . .

MARIE	This is a mistake.
TERRY	You what?
MARIE	I shouldn't have come. Night, Terry. No, I mean, goodbye.

She starts to walk away, as he follows her.

| TERRY | Hang on a minute. You've got your wires crossed . . . Marie? |

SCENE 7

The school gates. Ben is waiting for Clare to come out.

BEN	Hey, Clare. Come here. You been blabbing?
CLARE	What's that supposed to mean?
BEN	You know what I'm talking about. Little men in panda cars, who just happen to drop by my house. And Terry's. And Jason's.
CLARE	Nothing to do with me.

Terry comes up and joins them.

TERRY	Well?
BEN	She says not.
TERRY	Right, but do you believe her?
CLARE	Hey, what is this?
TERRY	This is me looking for a grass.
CLARE	But everyone knows. You've all been talking about it.
TERRY	Right. But we haven't all been talking to the law.
BEN	What about Marie?
TERRY	What about her?
BEN	Don't get me wrong, but sometimes . . .
TERRY	Yeah, she's been a bit funny. But she wouldn't . . . would she? You're her mate. What do you reckon?

CLARE	Well, you go out with her. Shouldn't think so, but . . . what do you want me to say?
TERRY	I want you to say what's happening. I want to know who grassed.

SCENE 8

We see both ends of a telephone conversation.

MUM	Ms Richards?
MS RICHARDS	Hello? Yes? Can I help you?
MUM	This is Mrs Colton, Marie's mum.
MS RICHARDS	Thank you for ringing. We've been worried about Marie.
MUM	Not as worried as me. But the worst's over now.
MS RICHARDS	So she will be coming back to school?
MUM	Well, yes. That's what I wanted to talk about. This business has been upsetting, but the quicker she gets back to normal –
MS RICHARDS	I couldn't agree more.
MUM	She's very tense. There's been rumours, a couple of threats.
MS RICHARDS	I'm sorry, did you say threats?
MUM	Well, you know. Boys acting tough.
MS RICHARDS	These are violent young men. It was a serious crime.
MUM	Of course. Marie knew there'd be trouble, if she was a witness. Now she just wants to get on with her life, go back to school –
MS RICHARDS	I'm not sure that's the best idea . . .
MUM	I beg your pardon?
MS RICHARDS	We do have the other pupils to consider.

MUM	But you just said –
MS RICHARDS	I know. I do sympathise, Mrs Colton, but if Marie's return puts other pupils at risk, then maybe it might be best to wait a bit –
MUM	But it's not her fault. She's done nothing wrong.
MS RICHARDS	I would still advise her to stay at home for now.
MUM	What about her exams? She needs to get back to work.
MS RICHARDS	Perhaps if you were to give me a ring next week?
MUM	You ought to be ashamed of yourself. Goodbye. (*Slams phone down.*)

SCENE 9

Marie is walking home. She stops, and turns round, but sees nothing. There is a noise, in the darkness. She turns towards it. After a pause, she runs home.

MUM	What's the rush? Are you OK?
MARIE	No. But I'm glad to be home.
MUM	What happened?
MARIE	Someone followed me.
MUM	It's a rough area. There's some lunatics about.
MARIE	Come off it, Mum. This is about Terry.
MUM	They're charging him?
MARIE	Yeah.
MUM	Will he plead guilty?
MARIE	I don't know. I hope so.
MUM	But if he doesn't?
MARIE	If he pleads not guilty I have to give evidence.
MUM	I hope it won't come to that . . .

MARIE	So do I, Mum. But I'll have to. I told them I would. That's what this is about, I know it.
	The phone rings, Mum answers.
MUM	Hello?
	From outside.
BEN	Can I speak to Marie?
	Mum hands the phone over.
MARIE	Hello, who is it?
BEN	Is that Marie?
MARIE	Yes?
BEN	You're dead. You testify, and you are dead.
MARIE	Yeah, right. (*Puts phone down.*)
MUM	What was it, love?
MARIE	Just a message.
MUM	I'm sorry.
MARIE	Are you? D'you wish I hadn't done it? Maybe Clare's got it sussed. Keep your mouth shut, stay alive.
MUM	No, it's not that. I'm proud of you, Marie, really I am. I just don't want you to get hurt.
MARIE	Oh, me too. Really, I'm no hero. And it's all your fault, Mum. The way you brought me up. I just can't help thinking about that lad. What if it was me, if that happened to me, and nobody came forward, nobody said . . .

Joyride

Steve Barlow and Steve Skidmore

List of Characters

Police officer
Woman/Mother
First youth
Second youth
Detective
Phil
Mum
Dad
Reporter
Eyewitness

NOTES

1 In this short script there are twelve scenes, which happen in
   five different locations. This can be done by using spotlights if
   you have them, or simply by the players 'freezing', and only
   coming to life when they speak.
2 There should be no gaps between the scenes, but the pauses
   within the scenes can be as long as you like.

POLICE OFFICER We'll have to ask you to make an identification.

*The woman weeps and shakes her head to show that
she can't.*

I'm sorry, we have to have a formal identification.
It'll only take a moment.

FIRST YOUTH (*panting*) Cor, thought the Plod had us that time.

SECOND YOUTH Yeah-hey, see Phil in the yellow Merc?
Pheeeooooow! (*Mimes how fast Phil was travelling.*)

FIRST YOUTH	Goin' like the clappers with that cop car right behind him.
SECOND YOUTH	Awesome! (*sobering*) Reckon he got away?
FIRST YOUTH	Yeah – course. He'll be OK.

DETECTIVE	Well, you've done it properly this time, haven't you, sunshine?
PHIL	(*after a long pause*) Is she . . . ?
DETECTIVE	You were doing seventy and hit her smack on. What do you think?

MUM	(*coming in from work*) All right, Jack? Oooh, it's bitter out there. Phil in?
DAD	He went out – said he was going to the pictures with a mate.
MUM	Out? What if he's . . . ? You shouldn't have let him go.

REPORTER	Can you tell me exactly what you saw?
EYEWITNESS	This big yellow car came screechin' round the corner with a police car after him – he was going miles too fast and he goes up on the pavement where the little girl was. Next thing I know she's flying through the air . . .

POLICE OFFICER	There's one thing – she couldn't have known anything about it, it was so sudden. She probably never felt a thing.
MOTHER	She was running to get home first . . . She always did that . . . (*She breaks down.*)

DAD	He promised he wasn't going to do that any more.
MUM	I don't like him goin' out at night.
DAD	You can't wrap them in cotton wool, you know.

PHIL	I never meant it to happen.
DETECTIVE	That makes it all right, does it?

FIRST YOUTH	He won't come now.
SECOND YOUTH	Give him five minutes.

MUM	Stealing cars! I've never stolen anything in my life!
DAD	You don't know he's gone stealing cars.
MUM	You should've kept him in!
DAD	I'm going to bed.

EYEWITNESS	You'll spell my name right, won't you? Berresford, with two 'e's and two 'r's.

The reporter stares at her.

Almost together.

FIRST YOUTH	I'm off.
DAD	Are you coming?
PHIL	It was an accident!
REPORTER	Berresford – two 'r's.

MOTHER   What'll I tell her dad?

General freeze. The police officer pats the mother on the shoulder and moves forward. At the same time, the detective turns from Phil in disgust and moves forward to meet the police officer. Both are tired and do not wish to talk. Long pause.

DETECTIVE   And they call it a 'joyride'.

Freeze or blackout.

Pressure Point

Anthony Masters

List of Characters

Jason
Karl
Mrs Samuels

Jason and Karl are standing in a darkened room. They are listening to footsteps coming down the stairs. Both boys are wearing balaclava masks.

JASON (*in a whisper*) Let's go back through the window.

KARL (*whispering as well*) No chance.

JASON (*getting desperate*) It was only a dare. We've got to get away.

KARL I told you – no chance. This has got to be worth doing.

JASON I never agreed to a burglary. I only agreed to a dare. I'm going.

KARL (*grabbing Jason's arm*) You're not going anywhere. An old lady lives here, right? She couldn't harm a flea.

JASON That's not the point.

They listen intently as the footsteps reach the foot of the stairs.
There is a tense silence.
Mrs Samuels, the old lady, is clearly listening.
So are Karl and Jason.
No one moves.
Then Mrs Samuels pushes open the sitting-room door and snaps on the light. She is holding a poker. When she sees Jason and Karl, Mrs Samuels gasps with fear.

For a moment they all stare at each other in horror.

MRS SAMUELS (*Her voice is shaking and she looks as if she might have a heart attack at any moment.*) What are you doing here? (*Neither Jason nor Karl replies.*) What are you *doing* here?

KARL (*with mock bravado*) Just hand over your valuables.

MRS SAMUELS What?

KARL You heard.

Mrs Samuels grips the poker harder, but now her hands are trembling.

MRS SAMUELS How dare you! Get out of my house. I'm not giving you anything.

KARL That's a pity. You could get hurt if you don't. (*But he doesn't sound very sure of himself.*)

JASON Come on. Let's go.

KARL Stay where you are.

Jason stays.

I'm not going to ask you again, lady. If you've got any money, or jewellery, hand it over or you'll be sorry. (*But he sounds even more uncertain.*)

MRS SAMUELS I'm going to ring the police.

JASON Come on, Karl. Let's get out of here.

MRS SAMUELS So it's Karl, is it?

KARL (*rounding on Jason*) You idiot! (*He turns back to Mrs Samuels.*) There are plenty of Karls in the world.

MRS SAMUELS I'm sure there are. (*Her voice is still very quavery, but she seems to have gained a little confidence.*) But the police will soon sort you out.

Jason begins to back off towards the open window, but Mrs Samuels moves surprisingly quickly and cuts him off. Still holding the poker, she grabs the phone.

JASON	Don't do that.
MRS SAMUELS	Why not? You've broken into my home.
JASON	(*clearly very afraid*) It was just a dare.
MRS SAMUELS	(*slightly thrown*) A what?
JASON	(*speaking very fast*) A dare. We keep daring each other. Like we dared each other to climb this high wall at the youth club.
KARL	Shut up, you raving idiot!
MRS SAMUELS	So you dared each other to break into my house and threaten me.
JASON	(*desperately trying to convince her*) We didn't mean to threaten you. We're not burglars. It was just a dare.
MRS SAMUELS	Who are you trying to impress?
JASON	Our girlfriends.
KARL	I told you to shut up. (*determined to be heavy*) We're not kids. This is a burglary. Do you get it?

Mrs Samuels picks up the receiver.

KARL	(*advancing on her*) Drop it!

Mrs Samuels rather ineffectively raises the poker as Karl continues to approach.

Get away from that phone!

She begins to dial.

Please, put down the receiver.

The word 'please' startles them all.

JASON	Please don't shop us.

Slowly and reluctantly, Mrs Samuels puts down the receiver, but she is still between Karl and Jason and the open window. Mrs Samuels staggers slightly.

	Are you OK?
MRS SAMUELS	(*clutching the table*) I'm fine.
JASON	Why don't you sit down?
MRS SAMUELS	No.
KARL	Why not?
MRS SAMUELS	Because you'll climb out of the window and escape.
KARL	Too right we will.
MRS SAMUELS	No, you won't. (*But she is clearly unwell.*)
JASON	You look ill. You should sit down.

Mrs Samuels, gasping for breath, collapses on a chair by the open window. She is still holding the poker but is now shaking all over.
Karl and Jason hesitate. They don't know what to do.

	Just let us go. We didn't mean any harm. I told you – it was a dare. A stupid dare.
MRS SAMUELS	(*staring at Karl*) You tried to rob me.
JASON	He didn't mean –
MRS SAMUELS	Be quiet. I'm talking to your friend. Not that he should be your friend if he led you on like this.
KARL	(*belligerently*) I didn't lead anyone on.
MRS SAMUELS	You tried to rob me. If I call the police you'll get a prison sentence.
KARL	We won't be hanging around for them to arrive.
MRS SAMUELS	You'll have left fingerprints. They'll find you.

KARL	I've had enough of this. I'm going through that window and if you try to stop me, you'll get hurt.
MRS SAMUELS	Of course I'll try to stop you. I have to protect myself. You've broken into my home and threatened to rob me.
KARL	Get out of the way. (*He tries to push past Mrs Samuels.*)

Mrs Samuels staggers to her feet and grabs at Karl's balaclava mask. Surprisingly, she manages to pull it off.

| MRS SAMUELS | Now I'll remember your face. Now I can give a description of you to the police. |

Karl stands exposed, looking childish and discomfited. Then he clenches his fists.

| KARL | You stupid old bat! I'll fix you. |

Mrs Samuels sits down again with a little cry of fear. She slumps in the chair and her eyes close.

JASON	You've done for her.
KARL	She's all right. Look, she's breathing.
JASON	Only just.
KARL	Let's go.
JASON	We can't leave her.
KARL	I told you, she's all right. There's nothing we can do.
JASON	(*bending over Mrs Samuels*) She could die.

Karl hesitates.

We'd be murderers.

| KARL | What can we do? |
| JASON | Call an ambulance. |

KARL	And then go?
JASON	We should wait till the ambulance comes, in case she needs help.
KARL	What can we do?
JASON	How do I know?

Mrs Samuels begins to revive, her eyes opening and staring up at the two boys.

MRS SAMUELS	Haven't you gone yet?
KARL	We thought you were sick.
MRS SAMUELS	I've got a heart condition. My pills are in my dressing-gown pocket. (*She seems unable to drag them out.*)

Karl rummages in her pocket and produces the bottle of pills.

KARL	How many do you take?
MRS SAMUELS	Just one.

Karl tips up the bottle and hands a pill to Mrs Samuels, who swallows it. There is a long silence.

KARL	You OK?
MRS SAMUELS	I'm feeling better.
KARL	Will you let us go?

He has completely changed his attitude and is no longer aggressive. Now it's as if they are Mrs Samuels's prisoners.

MRS SAMUELS	Why should I?
KARL	I'm sorry about what happened.
MRS SAMUELS	You don't care.
KARL	I do. My gran's about your age.

MRS SAMUELS	Would you try and rob her?
KARL	(*indignantly*) Of course not.
MRS SAMUELS	Then why me?
KARL	You were a stranger. I'm sorry. Can't you let us go? My mate's right. It was all a stupid dare. We're always competing against each other, winding each other up.
MRS SAMUELS	Why?
KARL	I don't know.
JASON	I do.
MRS SAMUELS	Well?
JASON	We're no good at school.
KARL	Come on –
JASON	It's true. We can't read.
KARL	Rubbish.
JASON	It's true. So we got to prove ourselves, haven't we? We don't want to be put down.
MRS SAMUELS	Who's putting you down?
KARL	Other kids. Teachers. My dad. His mum.
MRS SAMUELS	So breaking and entering an old lady's house is proving yourself?
	Neither of the boys replies.
	You're not getting away with this. (*Again, her trembling hand reaches for the phone, but this time Karl neither threatens nor intervenes.*)
KARL	Do what you've got to do.
JASON	Please don't. We haven't been in trouble with the law before.
MRS SAMUELS	(*hesitating*) You sure about that?

KARL	Yeah.
MRS SAMUELS	If I let you go, you'll only burgle someone else.
JASON	We won't. I swear we won't – on my mother's life.
MRS SAMUELS	What about my life?
JASON	Please.
KARL	Stop whining. Phone the police if you've got to. You've seen my face. We can take the grief.
JASON	I don't want to be nicked for this. (*He is close to breaking down.*)

Mrs Samuels picks up the phone and begins to dial. She looks up at Karl and Jason. Then she puts the receiver down.

MRS SAMUELS	(*pointing at the open window with sudden decision*) Go.
JASON	What?
KARL	You heard her. Let's go.

The two boys climb through the window. Jason goes first and then Karl. He looks back.

You've got guts, you have.

MRS SAMUELS	Are you going to break into another old lady's home?
KARL	We're not breaking in anywhere again.
MRS SAMUELS	Why not?
KARL	Because you've got guts.

He disappears through the window.
Mrs Samuels gets up slowly and walks to the door.
We hear her footsteps going up the stairs. They are slow and dragging.

At the Post Office

George Kulbacki and Di Timmins

List of Characters

Roger
Bruce

ROGER	Morning, Bruce.
BRUCE	Oh, morning, Roger.
ROGER	Lovely day.
BRUCE	It certainly is.
ROGER	Did you have a good weekend?
BRUCE	Smashing, thanks.
ROGER	Did you get away anywhere?
BRUCE	Yes, we did, as a matter of fact. Got over to the coast for a couple of days. Great fun.
ROGER	Chance for plenty of exercise?
BRUCE	Of course! Wouldn't be a proper weekend away without the chance to do a bit of running on the beach. Managed that every morning and evening. Went swimming a few times, too.
ROGER	Wasn't the water a bit cold?
BRUCE	Didn't even notice it, old chap. Quick in-and-out, a brisk rub-down with a rough towel and I was right as rain. Did you get away?
ROGER	Yes, we did, actually. Spent Sunday in the country. Had a marvellous five-mile trek in the morning, spent lunch-time in the beer garden of a charming village pub, and in the afternoon I played a few games of 'catch' with the boys. Then home in the car.
BRUCE	We both missed a bit of action round here over the weekend, apparently.

ROGER	Oh, really?
BRUCE	Yes. You know Max, from Henshaw Avenue?
ROGER	Oh yes, known him for years.
BRUCE	He was involved in a fight on the High Street on Saturday afternoon.
ROGER	Never!
BRUCE	It's true.
ROGER	I would never have said he was the fighting type.
BRUCE	Apparently he bumped into someone he didn't like, there were raised voices and the next thing the two of them were rolling around on the ground.
ROGER	Dear me! What happened?
BRUCE	Well, as you can imagine, Mrs Williams was furious. She was dreadfully embarrassed and just dragged him off home.
ROGER	He'll be in her bad books, then.
BRUCE	Grounded for a fortnight, I believe.

Pause.

ROGER	Well, you heard about the vicar, then?
BRUCE	No, what's he done now?
ROGER	Well, apparently, old Harriet took him for a bit of a frolic through the churchyard and they both ended up in the shrubbery.
BRUCE	Oh I say. That's terrible.
ROGER	Harriet ended up with a very thorny coat, I can tell you. You never know what that old lady is going to do next.

Pause.

BRUCE	(*calling*) Hello, Boris!
ROGER	(*calling*) Hello, Boris!

BRUCE	(*calling*) You're looking well!
ROGER	(*calling*) Getting on OK?
BRUCE	(*calling*) Nice to see you!
ROGER	(*calling*) See you soon!
BRUCE	Well, he's put on weight.
ROGER	I know. I can't believe it. He used to be so trim. Happens to a lot of them when they retire, you know, these active workers.
BRUCE	Yes, he was never happier than when he was down on that farm, seeing to those sheep.
ROGER	It could be something else, though.
BRUCE	What?
ROGER	Haven't you noticed that his type often seem to run to fat when they reach middle age?
BRUCE	I suppose you're right.
ROGER	Still, he always looks well groomed, even more so now he's retired.
BRUCE	Very smart. It's that black and white coat, I suppose.
ROGER	Probably – though I prefer brown myself.
BRUCE	Anyway, how's that younger brother of yours?
ROGER	Oh I'm afraid he's still a little wild from time to time. He ran away from home on Tuesday.
BRUCE	What, again?
ROGER	We found him three days later roaming around Squire Anderton's wood.
BRUCE	Did you manage to persuade him to come home?
ROGER	Eventually. He was a bit reluctant to get into the car, though.
BRUCE	Always was a spirited little fellow.

ROGER	Yes, he probably needs to change his diet now he's getting a bit older.
BRUCE	Oh look, activity at last. We appear to be leaving.
ROGER	Straight down to the butcher's as usual?
BRUCE	I hope so. With any luck we'll get beef on the bone.
ROGER	See you next pension day, then.
BRUCE	And you. Bye!

Home

Ken Campbell

List of Characters

Johnstone
Keith

JOHNSTONE	I'm glad my cold's better.
KEITH	Hmmmm.
JOHNSTONE	Nice to be just taking it easy at home, isn't it?
KEITH	Hmmmm.
JOHNSTONE	Just sitting on our nice sofa taking it easy. What's the matter?
KEITH	I don't know.
JOHNSTONE	You looked really panicky all of a sudden.
KEITH	There's – there's something slightly peculiar about this place.
JOHNSTONE	What do you mean 'this place' – it's our home.
KEITH	I know – but somehow I don't feel quite at home here.
JOHNSTONE	Don't you?
KEITH	No.
JOHNSTONE	Now you come to mention it, I don't feel quite at home either.
KEITH	It may sound ridiculous, but I've got a feeling that this isn't our home, Johnstone.
JOHNSTONE	Yes it is.
KEITH	What makes you so positive?
JOHNSTONE	It looks like our home.
KEITH	I'll agree there – it looks exactly like our home.
JOHNSTONE	So it is home.
KEITH	But is it?

JOHNSTONE	It must be.
KEITH	I submit it could be a cunning copy. Some person unknown – for whatever bizarre purpose – has had our home copied in every minute detail.
JOHNSTONE	But why?
KEITH	That's what I intend to find out.
JOHNSTONE	You mean you think we've been trapped? That this is some sort of cage?
KEITH	I certainly think we'd be fools to ignore that possibility.
JOHNSTONE	But why would anyone go to all that trouble. Look, everything is absolutely the same. Look, they've even put a pair of old pongy socks exactly like mine in the corner by the door, exactly like I bunged them last Sunday. Mind you, they are a bit pongier than I remembered. But mind you, they would get pongier over the week. They've been there nearly a week so the pong would have spread through in that time – wouldn't it?
KEITH	Would it, though?
JOHNSTONE	Yes, I think so.
KEITH	I submit it wouldn't. I submit we have discovered the one minuscule error in this Evil Genius's otherwise perfectly effected plan – socks would get less pongy not more pongy. The air circulating round them. There's quite a draught blows under that door and it would have lessened the pong not increased it.
JOHNSTONE	But even so – why go to all this trouble?
KEITH	So we don't panic.
JOHNSTONE	What's he gonna do to us?
KEITH	We can only imagine.

JOHNSTONE	I'm frightened.
KEITH	We must keep our heads in all this. Act coolly and rationally at all times. Even if we are in a panic the last thing we must do is let him know.
JOHNSTONE	I'm gonna try the door.
	Opens all right. We're definitely not shut in.
KEITH	It could be a further measure to keep us from panicking – he gives us the illusion of escape.
JOHNSTONE	This is our home. Your whole theory is based on the flimsy supposition that sock pong doesn't spread.
KEITH	Maybe you're right. *(pause)* Johnstone . . .
JOHNSTONE	What?
KEITH	I still don't feel fully at home.
JOHNSTONE	Well, I do.
KEITH	Are you sure?
JOHNSTONE	Yes.
KEITH	You can honestly say that you feel totally and fully at home?
JOHNSTONE	Yes.
KEITH	Johnstone – absolutely?
JOHNSTONE	Well, not absolutely.
KEITH	Heh!
JOHNSTONE	Yes, but I never feel absolutely at home – not even at home. So if I did feel *absolutely* at home at home that would mean it definitely wasn't home. And if you really want to know, I'll tell you why I never feel absolutely at home at home – it's you. It's because I never know from one minute to the next when you're liable to leap to some nutty conclusion like we're in the clutches of an Evil Genius who's made an exact copy of our home.

Keith laughs insanely.

What's so funny?

KEITH I am the Evil Genius, Johnstone! Haha! I know this isn't our home and that it's a replica because I built it! How do you think whoever it was was able to duplicate our humble abode in every detail? Surely it would be obvious to the dimmest of wits that only a man who actually lived in the house could duplicate it so exactly.

JOHNSTONE But look at me closely, Keith – only now am I permitted to reveal that I am not Johnstone!

KEITH What?

JOHNSTONE I am only a replica of Johnstone – a lifelike robot replica – completely identical in every detail. Johnstone uncovered your little scheme some weeks ago and while you were busy building this duplicate home he was at work on this duplicate Johnstone.

KEITH Yes, but I've known that all along.

JOHNSTONE What?

KEITH Do you think I didn't know what Johnstone was up to? Why, man, that's why I allowed him to uncover my scheme – I knew he'd immediately build a replica of himself and it's the replica I wanted.

JOHNSTONE What for?

KEITH To eat.

JOHNSTONE You're going to eat me?

KEITH Yes – you're only a replica.

JOHNSTONE Ow, get off – just a minute – Oh no!

KEITH What?

JOHNSTONE The replica of Johnstone was so incredibly like the original that he had difficulty telling them apart . . . So do you know what he's done?

KEITH	What?
JOHNSTONE	He's sent the real Johnstone to your duplicate house.
KEITH	You mean you are the real Johnstone?
JOHNSTONE	Yes, like a fool I've left my replica back at our real home.
KEITH	But this is our real home. All the time you thought I was building a duplicate home I was just down the pub. Haha! So you built a replica Johnstone all for nothing!
JOHNSTONE	Except I didn't build a replica Johnstone – while you were off at the pub thinking I was building a replica Johnstone I was off down the pictures with Gertie.
KEITH	Actually I made all that up.
JOHNSTONE	So did I. Even the bit about Gertie.
KEITH	Still the mystery of the socks.
JOHNSTONE	Oh, I had a cold, didn't I, that's why I don't remember them as being so pongy.
KEITH	Oh. Dull old life, isn't it?

Spies

Ken Campbell

List of Characters

Keith
Johnstone

KEITH	Right, Johnstone, we're spies now.
JOHNSTONE	Spies?
KEITH	Yes, that's our new job.
JOHNSTONE	Who gave us this job?
KEITH	I can't possibly tell you that.
JOHNSTONE	Why not?
KEITH	I don't know. Obviously he's not going to tell me who he is in case I get caught and tortured and give him away.
JOHNSTONE	So some bloke just popped up and said we've got to be spies now.
KEITH	Yes.
JOHNSTONE	Who've we got to spy on?
KEITH	The enemy.
JOHNSTONE	What enemy?
KEITH	I can't possibly tell you that.
JOHNSTONE	Cos you don't know.
KEITH	Cos *they* don't know.
JOHNSTONE	They don't know they're the enemy?
KEITH	No.
JOHNSTONE	If we don't know who they are and they don't even know they're them, anyway, how are we going to know if we're spying on the right ones?
KEITH	To begin with we suspect everyone. Even each other.

	Even ourselves. It's a tough assignment, Johnstone. That's why they've called us in. I shall now teach you today's code.
JOHNSTONE	Today's code.
KEITH	Today's code – to confuse the enemy. It's not enough for them not to know who they are, they mustn't know where they are either. To effect this confusion we shall talk at all times in opposites. We shall practise that now. Are you ready?
JOHNSTONE	Yes.
KEITH	So you're not ready?
JOHNSTONE	No, I am.
KEITH	Haha! I'd started already! Opposites, Johnstone! If you mean long you say short, if you mean short you say long. If you mean left you say right, if you mean right you say wrong. If you mean delightful odour you say 'orrible pong. Got it?
JOHNSTONE	Yes.
KEITH	Yes!
JOHNSTONE	Yes.
KEITH	So you haven't got it.
JOHNSTONE	No, I have.
KEITH	So you haven't.
JOHNSTONE	I have.
KEITH	Opposites! If you have got it you say you haven't got it. Have you got it?
JOHNSTONE	No!
KEITH	That's bad!
JOHNSTONE	Why's that bad?
KEITH	It's good so I say it's bad!

Keith clouts Johnstone.

JOHNSTONE	Ow! All right there's no need to hurt. I think it's a soppy code and I'm not going to speak in it. It's not going to fool anyone, it's just soppy. We'll just get locked up again for acting batty.
KEITH	No we won't.
JOHNSTONE	Ah! So we will.
KEITH	What?
JOHNSTONE	Opposites! You said we won't get locked up so that means we will!
KEITH	I wasn't talking in code then.
JOHNSTONE	So you *were*!
KEITH	I mean yes I was.
JOHNSTONE	That's what I thought.
KEITH	Shut up!
JOHNSTONE	(*loudly*) Yahoooo! Rootytoot!
KEITH	I mean make a racket! Thank you no thank you. If I am not talking in opposites I shall go 'Thppppp!' first and then you will know that I did mean that.
JOHNSTONE	So that's what you won't do.
KEITH	That's what I will do.
JOHNSTONE	Well you should have gone 'Thppppp!' first then. You don't seem to have much of a grip on this code.
KEITH	Listen! I'm going batty! I mean stuff up your ears! Thppppp! If I am not talking in opposites I shall go 'Thppppp!' first and then you will know that I did mean that! Thppppp! Is that clear?
JOHNSTONE	Thppppp! Yes.
KEITH	Thppppp! Good.

JOHNSTONE	Thppppp! This going 'Thppppp!' is more fun than opposites, isn't it?
KEITH	Thppppp! Yes.
JOHNSTONE	Thppppp! (*Pause*)
KEITH	Thppppp! You mustn't go 'Thppppp!' if you haven't got anything to say.
JOHNSTONE	Thppppp! Why not?
KEITH	Thppppp! Well, I think you're going to say something.
JOHNSTONE	Thppppp! But you soon find out I'm not when I don't.
KEITH	Thppppp! True. Thppppp! We'll jack in that opposites notion and stick to thpppping, shall we?
JOHNSTONE	Thppppp! Won't that man be cross?
KEITH	Thppppp! What man?
JOHNSTONE	Thppppp! That man who gave us the job of spies.
KEITH	Oh I made that up, actually.
JOHNSTONE	Why?
KEITH	Bored. Nothing ever really happens, does it?
JOHNSTONE	I suppose we better go to bed, then.
KEITH	Not just now – I've got a funny feeling coming on.

The Off-side Trap

Mary Colson

List of Characters

Maxine
Maxine 1 (her thoughts)
Paul
Paul 1 (his thoughts)
Dave (Paul's friend)
Shelly (Maxine's friend)

NOTES

Dave and Shelly can be read by Maxine 1 and Paul 1.

SETTING

Football club disco.

Maxine really fancies Paul and he quite likes her. They're thirteen years old. He's hugely into football – she knows nothing about it but has to pretend she does in order to make conversation. While their thoughts are being spoken, Maxine and Paul are experiencing awkward silences, looking ill at ease and searching for something to say. There is a prevailing embarrassed awkwardness throughout their dialogue.

MAXINE	Hi, Paul.
MAXINE 1	OK, done it. Made contact.
PAUL	All right, Maxine.
MAXINE 1	He doesn't sound very pleased to see me.
PAUL	What you up to?
PAUL 1	Tell me I didn't say that – talk about stating the blinking obvious!
MAXINE	Oh, you know, nothing much.
PAUL	Right.

Pause.

| MAXINE 1 | Come on, come on. Say something. |
| PAUL 1 | What do I say now? |

Pause.

PAUL	So . . . um . . .
MAXINE	(*at the same time*) What did you . . . Oh, sorry.
MAXINE 1	Oh no – how clumsy was that?
PAUL	No, you first.
PAUL 1	Come on, man, be cool.
MAXINE	I was just going to ask what you did today. Did you play?
MAXINE 1	That's better. More confident. Dead cas.
PAUL	Yeah. Well, I was sub.
PAUL 1	I sound like a half-wit! I haven't said a normal sentence yet. What's she going to think?
MAXINE	I see. Whereabouts did you play, then? On the wing?
MAXINE 1	Did that sound technical enough? Do you even have wings in footie? I wish I'd listened to our Stuart when he used to go on.
PAUL	No, I went on for Dave in midfield.
PAUL 1	A sentence! At last!
MAXINE	Good match, was it?
MAXINE 1	Smooth.
PAUL	Not really, we lost 3–1.

Pause.

MAXINE	Oh, sorry.
MAXINE 1	Why'd I have to put my foot in it?
PAUL 1	Oh God! What now?
MAXINE	So do you play in a league or something?

MAXINE 1	This is awful.
PAUL	Yeah, but it's nothing great or anything. It's just a local Saturday league.
PAUL 1	Is she as bored as I am?
MAXINE 1	This has to be the most boring conversation I've ever had.
MAXINE	So do you want to dance? I like this one.
MAXINE 1	Anything to avoid talking!
PAUL	I'm not much good at dancing, actually.
PAUL 1	I can't dance at all – nightmare. I'm not having Gav and that lot laughing at me – no way.
MAXINE	Neither am I really – Shelly always says I've got one dance that I do whatever the song is. I don't think that's true but she says it is.
MAXINE 1	I really like this one – I might just go and join Shell and Rach anyway if he won't dance with me.
	Pause.
MAXINE	What sort of music do you like?
MAXINE 1	He must like *some* music – even if it's heavy metal.
PAUL	I like rap, you know, Eminem and such.
PAUL 1	That sounds pretty cool.
MAXINE	Isn't he the one who's been done for attacking somebody?
MAXINE 1	Oh, I can't stand rap! Even heavy metal would've been better than rap.
PAUL	Yeah, but that's just the way it is in America – you just have to accept it.
PAUL 1	She must think I'm pretty cool now.
MAXINE	What? You have to accept people killing each other?
MAXINE 1	I can't believe he's saying this.

PAUL 1	Oh here we go – what is it with girls and violence? It's not as if it's really happening, is it?
PAUL	It's just the way it is in the States, Maxine, it's the law of the gun.
PAUL 1	She'll soon see I'm right.
MAXINE	I'm sorry, Paul, but I don't think it's fun to point guns at people or beat them up. It's barbaric.
MAXINE 1	How naïve can he be?
PAUL 1	Oh God.
PAUL	So you don't ever watch anything violent at all?
MAXINE	No, I don't.
PAUL	I expect you watch *EastEnders* and *Neighbours* and stuff though, don't you?
MAXINE	Yeah, who doesn't?
PAUL	What about the explosions they had at the car yard and all the slagging off they do?
MAXINE 1	What's he getting at? What's he saying?
MAXINE	Well, yeah, but it's only a story, isn't it? It's not real.
PAUL 1	Is she thick or what?
PAUL	But it's supposed to reflect society so it seems like it's real.
MAXINE	I suppose so.
PAUL 1	At last! She's starting to get the picture. Cor, took her a while.
MAXINE 1	I don't get this. Does he think it's real people?
PAUL	And when you think about it, they've had murders, crimes, assaults, drugs – all the things that happen in real life.
MAXINE	Yeah, so?
PAUL	So it's not just in America that it's violent – it's here too, it's just we don't have as many guns.

PAUL 1	Made it!
MAXINE 1	Wow, that's a really thoughtful thing to say.
MAXINE	You've got a really mature attitude towards things, Paul.
PAUL 1	I'm in here.
MAXINE 1	He's so nice and mature – not like those silly boys who talk about gangs and guns all the time.
PAUL	Yeah, well, you've got to, haven't you?
PAUL 1	Go on, my son!
MAXINE	Yeah.
MAXINE 1	He's gorgeous.
PAUL 1	She's all right is Maxine. Dave'll be dead jealous.
MAXINE 1	I've got to tell Shell, she'll be so envious!
MAXINE AND PAUL	I've just got to . . .
PAUL	Oh, sorry. After you.
MAXINE 1	He's such a gentleman!
MAXINE	I was just going to ask you if you could hold my coke whilst I go to the loo.
MAXINE 1	How embarrassing! I hate my bladder.
PAUL	Oh yeah, sure.
MAXINE	I'll be back in a sec.
PAUL	Right.

Maxine leaves Paul and walks over to Shelly who's standing near the girls' toilets. Paul remains where he is and his friend Dave comes over.

MAXINE	Oh, Shell, I spoke to him! He's absolutely gorgeous!
SHELLY	What'd he say? It looked like you were getting on really well.
MAXINE	Oh, you know, we just talked about telly and stuff.

SHELLY	Well? Are you going out with him or what?
MAXINE	Well he hasn't asked me yet but . . .

DAVE	How's it going with the lovely Maxine, then?
PAUL	All right, actually. She is pretty stunning, isn't she?
DAVE	I'll say, she's a babe. What were you talking about? You've been chatting for ages.
PAUL	Oh, you know, footie, telly – the usual sort of stuff.
DAVE	Get in there, my man!
PAUL	Shut up, Dave, she's coming back.
DAVE	See you later, Romeo.

MAXINE	Hiya.
MAXINE 1	He looks different somehow.
PAUL	Hi.
PAUL 1	Dave's right; she *is* a babe.
MAXINE	Thanks for holding my drink.
PAUL	No worries.

A beat.

	So . . . uh . . . Do you want to dance? I'm not very good, like I said, but if you want to . . .
PAUL 1	Oh God, please say no!
MAXINE	No, that's OK. I'm happy just talking.
PAUL	Well, if that's what you want, that's fine with me.

They smile happily at each other.

MAXINE	I think we're really similar, don't you?
PAUL	Yeah, I suppose we are.
MAXINE	I mean, we've got similar friends, like the same sorts of things, music and stuff. We even hang around the same places.

PAUL	Yeah.
	A beat.
	Um . . . Maybe we could um . . . go out some time – to the cinema – um . . . There's a really good new film out – the one with Leonardo DiCaprio and um . . . Jennifer Aniston, I think.
MAXINE	I'd love to go.
MAXINE 1	Leo's so sweet!
PAUL	Great.
PAUL 1	Jennifer Aniston's such a stunner.
MAXINE	I've wanted to see it for ages.
PAUL	But it's only been out about a week.
MAXINE	Oh, well, I've read loads about it – it sounds really good.
MAXINE 1	I can't believe he wants to see this film. Most lads hate Leo.
PAUL	Yeah, I think it's good to see all sorts of different films.
MAXINE	Mm. When do you want to go?
PAUL	How about tomorrow night?
MAXINE	Great.
MAXINE 1	Fantastic – a night with Paul and Leo!
PAUL 1	I can't believe it – I get to see Jennifer Aniston and Maxine at the same time! And I get to see Leonardo DiCaprio looking a right idiot pretending to be an ugly midfielder – I bet he can't even kick the ball straight. I'm a genius!
MAXINE 1 AND PAUL 1	Cool.

Date

Ann Cartwright

List of Characters

Two characters with no name

1   Rule One of going out on a date is, be cool.

2   Oh. I thought Rule One was have a wash.

1   Well, yes of course. Having a wash goes without saying. Then, be cool.

2   I thought it was, have a wash, comb your hair, wear something clean and don't say anything stupid.

1   That's Rule Two.

2   What? The comb-your-hair bit?

1   No. The what-to-wear bit. Nothing bright.

2   Luminous, you mean?

1   In your case, yes. Do *not* go out wearing that luminous green shirt.

2   Not even with the shiny red boots with the stars on them?

1   No. Black is a good colour for dates. Very cool.

2   The only thing I've got to wear that's black is that T-shirt.

1   Oh. That's not bad, that one.

2   Except I dropped bleach down it cleaning the sink the other day.

1   Oh.

2   So it looks like a meteorite hit me.

1   Oh. We'll have a look in your wardrobe later. Rule Three is the don't-say-anything-stupid bit.

2   Right.

1   It's very important not only to look cool, but to talk cool.

2   So, what should I talk about, then?

1	Something that interests you. Which would be what?
2	Well, I think water is very interesting.
1	Water?
2	Yes. I think it's interesting the way water goes down the plug-hole – but always in the same direction.
1	Down, you mean.
2	Clockwise.
1	I see.
2	And I think it's really interesting the way it falls in bits from the sky.
1	Drops.
2	That as well. And when you put it in the freezer, it goes hard and you can make ice-lollies out of it.
1	And you think that this will interest your date, do you?
2	I don't know. Do you think it's a bit – intense to start off with? To break the ice with? Oh! Break the ice! That's a joke, isn't it? Wait a sec. I'll write that down.
1	Do you have anything else you're interested in?
2	Potatoes.
1	Oh dear.
2	Isn't it funny? It doesn't matter what you do to them – mash them, boil them, fry them, drop them on the floor – they still taste nice.
1	What about music? Do you like music?
2	Yes.
1	What kind?
2	Anything on the radio, really.
1	Like who?
2	Oh, I don't know, really. Thingy.
1	Who?

2 Thingy. He's good, he is. You know. The one that plays with Doo-Dah.

1 Thingy and Doo-Dah.

2 I'm not very good at remembering names. Oh! And Wotsit. I like her as well.

1 It's really important that you don't talk stupid to your date. Like about Thingy and Doo-Dah.

2 And Wotsit.

1 And Wotsit.

2 Why?

1 Because they'll run off.

2 Oh. That'd be no good, would it?

1 No. And you do need to talk a lot to your date, because that's Rule Four. Find out something that you've got in common.

2 But I already know something that we've got in common.

1 Do you? Great! What is it?

2 We're both dense.

1 Excellent! No worries, then.

2 So, shall I wear the black T-shirt with the bleach all over it?

1 Absolutely.

2 And talk about spuds, Thingy and Doo-Dah?

1 And don't forget Wotsit.

2 Wotsit! Of course! Thanks for reminding me. I'll just write that down. It's been a big help talking to you.

1 Not at all.

2 By the way . . . Should I kiss on the first date?

1 Why not? But only the feet.

2 Feet? I'm not that dense.

Bright Lights

David Calcutt

List of Characters

Storyteller
Helen
Gary
Nick

> *The main thoroughfare of the busy, bustling city. Night. A place of restaurants, multiplex cinemas, clubs, theatres, traffic, and so on.*
>
> *Storyteller is there, standing in the doorway of a nightclub, as a bouncer. Speaks to the audience.*
>
> *He turns and looks down the street a little way, to where Helen and Gary are walking. Our attention switches to them.*

STORYTELLER The city at night. Bright lights, music, hurry and hustle, bustle and rush. You can feel the excitement tingling in the air, the thrill of it shivering under your skin, the rhythm thumping up through the soles of your feet. All the promise of a good night out, if you know what you're looking for, and if you've got the money to pay for it. But if you haven't, and if you don't – if you're new to the city and don't know your way – well, it's a dangerous place, and you can end up lost for ever.

HELEN What shall we do, then?

GARY I don't know. Anything.

HELEN How much have you got?

GARY Thirty pounds.

HELEN We could go and see a film.

GARY See a film?

HELEN Yes –

GARY We can do better than that.

HELEN Like what?

GARY I don't know. Look around you. It's all here. Anything!

Attention switches back to Storyteller.

STORYTELLER Helen and Gary, sister and brother, out in the late-night city for the first time in their little lives. The products of a broken home. And who isn't these days? They live with their mother, and Friday nights they go and stay with their father. Only this Friday night, they haven't.

Attention switches to Gary and Helen.

HELEN We should've gone to Dad's.

GARY What for? So we can stay in and watch telly while he gets drunk down the pub?

HELEN He'll wonder where we are.

GARY No, he won't. He don't know what day of the week it is half the time.

HELEN All the same –

GARY Look, we'll go there. But later. After we've had some fun.

Attention switches to Storyteller.

STORYTELLER It's fun they're after. Fun and games and thrills and spills. But they won't find it here.

Gary and Helen are standing outside Storyteller's club. He turns to them.

	Want something?
GARY	How much does it cost to go in?
STORYTELLER	In here?
GARY	Yes.
STORYTELLER	More than you can afford.
GARY	How much?
STORYTELLER	Beat it.
GARY	Look, just tell us –
STORYTELLER	I'll tell you this. You're crowding the pavement. Causing an obstruction. And if you don't remove yourself, I'll have you removed. Understand?
GARY	You can't make us move –
STORYTELLER	You want a bet?
HELEN	Gary –
GARY	We've got money –
STORYTELLER	Push off!
HELEN	Come on, Gary. He means it. Come on! (*She pulls Gary away.*)
STORYTELLER	Go home and go to bed. This ain't no place for you.

Gary and Helen go. Storyteller speaks to us.

I'm only trying to do them a favour. Places like this can be dangerous for young innocents like them. And there's worse places than this. Places where real beasts lurk and live, if you know what I mean. Turn off the main way, and you'll find them, down in the dark alleys and side streets, creatures that live in the shadows, things that live on human flesh. If you know what's good for you, you'll keep away from them. Cos behind the bright lights there's darkness and . . . horror. And some people just don't know what's good for them.

Attention switches to Gary and Helen. They have moved down the street a little way and are standing outside a Chinese restaurant.

HELEN   How about something to eat? I'm starving.

GARY   In there, you mean?

HELEN   I love Chinese food.

GARY   We can find a take-away.

HELEN   It's not the same. I've never ate in a restaurant before. Becky from school went to one for her birthday and she said –

GARY   Have you seen these prices?

HELEN   We can afford it. Just about.

GARY   And have nothing left.

HELEN   You got any better ideas?

GARY   Maybe.

Helen looks at the menu. As she does, Gary moves away.

HELEN   We could have that . . . and that . . . or that . . . Oh, come on, Gary, please –

She turns. Gary has walked off. She runs after him.

Gary . . . Where are you going . . . ?

Switch to Storyteller.

STORYTELLER   Off the main way, down the dark street, straight into the devil's den.

Switch to Gary and Helen. They have turned off the main thoroughfare and are walking down a dark side street.

HELEN	What are we doing down here?
GARY	Looking.
HELEN	Looking for what?
GARY	Fun.
HELEN	Down here? There's nothing down here.
GARY	Yes, there is.
HELEN	I don't like it. It's dark. It doesn't feel . . . safe . . .
GARY	Scared, are you?
HELEN	Yes! I am!
GARY	What of?
HELEN	I don't know. You read things.
GARY	Go on, then. Go back. Go to Dad's. Here's five pounds. That'll get you there. (*He offers her the money. She just looks at it.*) Ten, then. (*He takes out another five pounds, shoves the two notes into her hand.*) Go on, if you're going! Clear off!
HELEN	On my own?
GARY	Yes.
HELEN	What about you?
GARY	I'll see you there later.
HELEN	You won't find anything down here, Gary.
GARY	Yes, I will. See you.

Gary turns and walks off. Helen watches as he recedes into the darkness of the street. She looks at the money in her hand, turns, and walks back up the alley towards the main thoroughfare. We hear Storyteller's voice.

STORYTELLER	Bright lights, loud music, a sweet smell in the air – the smell of death.

Attention switches to Gary, in the side street. He stands before a lit doorway above which there hangs a sign, 'The Gingerbread Club'. He reads the name aloud.

GARY　'The Gingerbread Club'.

A voice whispers suddenly nearby.

NICK　Hey!

Gary turns. Nick emerges from a shadow by the side of the doorway. He smiles broadly.

Want to go in?

He holds out his hand.

My name's Nick.

Gary stares at Nick.

Be friendly.

Gary shakes Nick's hand. Nick does not let go.

You want to go in there?

GARY　What is it?

NICK　You can read, can't you?

GARY　'The Gingerbread Club'. But what is it?

NICK　The place where your dreams come true.

Gary pulls his hand away from Nick's grasp.

GARY　You're having me on –

He turns away. Nick moves in front of him, still smiling.

NICK　I can promise you a good time. Really good, I mean. That's what you're after, isn't it? Something . . . special. It's special in there, all right.

GARY   What's so special about it?

NICK   Go in and find out.

Gary is still hesitant.

How about a taste?

Nick goes up to the door, opens it. We hear music playing from inside, glimpse a flash of bright, coloured lights. The sight and the sound seem to entrance Gary.

A place of enchantment and delight. Everything you could wish for. And when I say everything . . . You know what I mean?

Gary is still staring at the lights.

Still, if you're not interested. (*Nick closes the door.*)

GARY   No – I didn't say that – but . . . how much does it cost?

NICK   How much?

GARY   To get in.

NICK   How much have you got?

GARY   Twenty pounds.

NICK   Twenty pounds? Oh, that'll do. That'll do very nicely. More than enough, both for the entrance, and the extras.

GARY   What extras?

NICK   A little bit of spice to make it all nice. (*Nick holds out some pills in his hand.*) It's the extras that make it special.

GARY   What are they?

NICK   They're so new they haven't got a name yet. Call them what you like. Sweeties. Dream-drops. Try one. On the house.

GARY   I don't know . . .

Nick speaks, still smiling, but with more force.

NICK   Try one!

Our attention switches to Storyteller.

STORYTELLER   So there he stands at hell's mouth, teetering on
              the edge, ready to fall in. And no one to help him.
              No one to take him by the hand, turn him round,
              guide him back. (*He turns and speaks to Helen, who is
              standing near him.*) Is there?

HELEN   What?

STORYTELLER   Where's your brother?

HELEN   My brother? How did you know – ?

STORYTELLER   You look alike. Lost him, have you?

HELEN   No –

STORYTELLER   Yes, you have. Or you will do if you don't hurry.
              Lose him for good.

HELEN   What do you mean?

STORYTELLER   You might be in time, if you hurry.

HELEN   Go after him. Back . . . down there . . . ?

STORYTELLER   Isn't he worth it? Your own brother? Isn't he worth
              the risk and the danger?

HELEN   Yes . . .

STORYTELLER   Go on, then. Go on!

Helen turns. Storyteller sniffs.

I can smell something cooking – and it's not the
Chinese restaurant.

*Attention switches to Gary and Nick outside the club.
Gary has taken one of the pills. He is losing control of
himself.*

NICK	Well?
GARY	Wow!
NICK	All right?
GARY	Yeah!
NICK	Was I right?
GARY	Yeah! Right!
NICK	Takes you up, eh?
GARY	Way up!
NICK	Higher and higher!
GARY	Yeah! Yeah!
NICK	Feel that tingling in your fingers, eh? Feel that heat in your bones. And that's only a taste. Only a little taste. In there, it gets hotter. In there, it'll burn you right up!
GARY	Let's go!
NICK	You ready?
GARY	I'm ready. Yeah!
NICK	Be my guest.

Nick opens the door. Music and lights again. Gary steps up. Nick stops him, holds out his hand.

Pay up.

GARY	Oh, yeah.

He gives Nick all his money. Nick steps aside.

NICK	After you.

Gary steps into the doorway.

GARY	It's great. It's like . . . like . . . I don't know . . .
NICK	An oven?
GARY	What?

Nick laughs.

Yeah! Like an oven! Yeah!

He's about to step in when Helen calls.

HELEN   Gary!

Gary turns, sees Helen. He's framed in the doorway with light.

What are you doing? Where are you going?

GARY   To paradise. (*to Nick*) Right?

NICK   Right.

HELEN   Don't, Gary. You don't know what's in there. It can't be good, whatever it is. Not down here.

GARY   But it is, Helen. It is good!

HELEN   It's not! Come on, Gary. Let's go. Please. Let's just go home!

Gary seems to hesitate for a second, then he turns, and disappears into the light.

No!

She takes a step forward. Nick closes the door.

NICK   Sorry. Too late. (*Nick takes a threatening step towards her.*) Get lost, little girl. Push off. If you know what's good for you. You get my meaning? (*He comes closer to her.*) Unless you want to go in after him. But it'll cost you!

HELEN   No . . . no . . .

She backs off, turns, and runs down the side street into the dark. Nick looks after her, grinning.

NICK   Never mind. Another time, maybe. (*He turns and walks back into the shadows.*)

STORYTELLER   So she runs, and leaves him to . . . whatever waits for him in there. Will she ever know? Will she ever see him again?

Probably not. He's just another child taken by the big city, swallowed up and lost for ever. Another child who vanished into the dark behind the bright lights. Of course, if this was a fairytale, she'd have gone in there and saved him, and they'd have gone back home, and lived happily ever after. If this was a fairytale. But it isn't.

The Mortgage

Chris Burgess

List of Characters

Amanda, the daughter of the family, and a very awkward child she is, both mentally and physically – though she has a turn of wit. Her legs are long and clad in black stockings. She is wearing a short gym-slip and blouse. On the top of her head she wears a large bow of ribbon of a violent colour. She is the caricature of a schoolgirl.

Sara, the mother of the family. She looks haggard and worn, and she whines rather than speaks. Her dress is that of a very poverty-stricken housewife.

John, the careworn father. He is dressed as a farmer, well-patched and mended.

Amelia, the damsel in distress. She is dressed in shabby clothes, with an old-fashioned bonnet. She is pale-faced and very sweet.

Richard, one of the sons. He is a prosperous, businessman type, with a corpulence to indicate good feeding. He wears a fur coat and a wide-brimmed hat.

Adolphus, the other son, a desperate-looking villain. He is dressed as a convict, and is badly in need of a wash and a shave. He should speak with a tough American accent of the cinema variety.

NOTES

1   The play is based on Stephen Leacock's story 'Caroline's Christmas' from *Nonsense Novels.*

2   All gestures, movements and emotions in the play should be deliberately exaggerated, and the lines should be spoken in a highly dramatic manner. It is the sort of play in which the characters can really let themselves go, and the more they do so, the greater the fun for all concerned.

The scene is the living-room of a small cottage. It is very poorly furnished. Left: a rough single bed with one tattered blanket. Centre: a kitchen chair. Right and beside the fireplace: two battered kitchen chairs. Over the fireplace there is a large, ornate 'HOME SWEET HOME'. The time is Christmas Eve.

Sara and Amanda are sitting huddled together by the dying embers of a log fire. They are obviously very cold.

AMANDA   The fire has almost gone out, Mother.

SARA   Yes, Amanda, the fire has almost gone out.

AMANDA   Let me put another log on it, Mother.

SARA   No, Amanda, it is the last log. We must wait 'til your father returns.

AMANDA   But, Mother, if Father is much longer even the embers will have died.

SARA   It is all right, my dear, I have one match left in the box. (*She rattles the matchbox.*)

AMANDA   I am hungry, Mother.

SARA   I know you are hungry, my dear. I am hungry, too. So is your father. So is Tiddles the cat.

AMANDA   Think of it, Mother, Christmas Eve and no milk for Tiddles.

SARA   Clara the cow has stopped giving milk since the snow covered the pasture. There is no food for Clara and no milk for Tiddles.

AMANDA   Mother, what is a mortgage?

SARA   Well, it's a sort of . . . a . . . Oh, really, child, it is much too complicated to explain. Ask your teacher after the holiday.

AMANDA   But, Mother, why do we have to leave our home at midnight tonight?

| SARA | Because your father owes five hundred pounds to the Farmstead Development Company, and if he cannot pay it by twelve o'clock they will take our home instead. These things always happen on Christmas Eve, especially when it is snowing. |

Footsteps at door left.

That will be your father.

Amanda opens the door. John enters and follows Amanda into the room. He is carrying a log and something wrapped in newspaper. His shoulders are bowed and he drags his feet wearily along the floor.

| AMANDA | Father! |
| JOHN | Amanda! |

Sara stands and flings her arms wide.

| SARA | John! |

John welcomes his wife in the same dramatic manner.

| JOHN | Sara! Sara, I have found a log! |

John holds out the log with a large gesture. Sara and Amanda gasp with pleasure.

SARA	And the book, John? Did you sell the book?
JOHN	Alas, my dear. Nobody wanted to buy *Mental Arithmetic Book 2*. No, not even with the answers. (*He takes the book from inside his coat.*)
SARA	Perhaps it is as well, John, it is the last book left in the house.
JOHN	The old place would not have been the same without it. Here, Amanda, place it back on the mantelpiece.

John gives Amanda the book, and she does as directed.

That's better. And here, Amanda, put the second last log on the fire. I'm cold and hungry and very tired.

John gives Amanda the log and she places it on the fire. John drags the chair at centre up to the fire and sits down. Amanda sits down, so that the three members of the family are sitting down together before the fire.

AMANDA   I am hungry, Father. Have you brought nothing to eat? I am so hungry I could even eat a school dinner.

SARA   Really, child, you can't be that hungry.

JOHN   Amanda, my dear, your old father has not failed you. (*He unwraps the newspaper parcel.*) I found these good things in the bins behind the restaurant in the village.

AMANDA   Oh, Father, what have you got?

JOHN   (*showing the food*) Look my dear! Three doughnuts, and one of them without a bite mark to be seen. Two lamp chops with quite a bit of meat left on them. A half-full packet of dehydrated carrots and some chips, cold but nutritious.

AMANDA   Oh, Father, may I have the doughnut without the bite mark?

JOHN   (*giving it to her*) Of course, my dearest daughter.

SARA   Amanda, eat it slowly.

But Amanda wolfs it down.

John, what time is it?

John takes out a very large watch. The chain is also ponderous.

JOHN   It is past eleven, Sara. Let us spend the last moments in our old home sitting round the fire. The bailiffs will be here in less than an hour.

| SARA | If only Richard and Adolphus were here, I'm sure they could have found the money to pay the mortgage. |

There is a knock at the door.

AMANDA	Perhaps that will be one of them.
JOHN	I doubt it, daughter. It is a long time since either of your brothers knocked at the door of their old home. (*John goes to the door.*)
SARA	It may be the bailiffs. Perhaps they have come early.
AMANDA	Their watches may be fast.

John opens the door. Amelia appears in the doorway. She is carrying a baby, well wrapped in a shawl.

| AMELIA | Excuse me, but I am looking for shelter. May I come in? |
| JOHN | Of course. You are very welcome. |

Enter Amelia. John closes the door. Sara stands and moves across to Amelia.

| SARA | You are cold, my child. Come, sit by the fire. |

Amelia sits.

AMELIA	I am very grateful.
AMANDA	Shall I take the baby? Your arms must be tired.
AMELIA	Thank you. (*She gives the baby to Amanda, who handles it very roughly.*)
AMANDA	I will warm it. (*She holds the baby very close to the fire.*)
JOHN	Careful, Amanda.

It is obvious that the shawl has started to smoulder, for Amanda snatches it away, turns the baby upside-down and pats it vigorously.

| AMELIA | Yes, please be careful, that's the only shawl I've got. |

SARA	And now, my dear, who are you, and why do you wander the frozen roads with your baby?
AMELIA	My name is Amelia. Some time ago my husband was sent to jail. A few days ago I spent my last penny on a rusk for the baby. There was no money for the rent. The landlord turned me into the street. Oh, woe is me, lackaday and botheration. (*She sobs.*)
JOHN	There, there, my dear! Amanda, get our visitor something to warm her up.
AMANDA	Yes, Father, I had better put the baby in a safe place. (*Amanda shoves the baby into the cupboard left, and then goes out.*)
AMELIA	Poor unhappy me! My husband in jail and no roof to my baby's head! Ah, me!
SARA	What is your baby's name, Amelia?
AMELIA	My baby hasn't got a name. My husband went to jail just before the baby was born, and I was never much good at thinking of names. I just call it Baby.

Enter Amanda with a tumbler of water. She picks up a doughnut.

AMANDA	Here is some food and drink. Take it.
AMELIA	You are very kind. (*She takes the offerings.*)
AMANDA	We wondered who it might be when you knocked.
SARA	Yes, we thought it might be one of my two sons.
AMELIA	You were expecting them?
JOHN	Both our sons left home many years ago.
SARA	You see, my first son said in his last letter that he finds it very hard to get away.
AMELIA	Oh, and where is he?
AMANDA	Dartmoor.

John and Sara make frantic attempts to silence their daughter, but she gabbles on.

He's doing ten years. He hit a night-watchman on the head with a piece of old iron. My brother has a good aim. The night-watchman was asleep for a long time, wasn't he, Father?

JOHN	Amanda, please!
AMELIA	And your other son?
JOHN	Richard went away five years ago.
SARA	He said he would not return until he had made a million pounds.
AMANDA	He may be a long time.
JOHN	He may never come.
SARA	He may be dead.

Sara and Amanda dissolve in tears in an embrace.

AMELIA	Oh, come, come, you mustn't talk like that. It depends on how clever Richard is, and how he went about making money.
AMANDA	His brother tried to make money. He went the wrong way about it.
JOHN	Drink up, Amelia, there's nothing like a glass of water when you're feeling low.

Amelia sips the water. As she does so she heaves a great sigh and faints. John catches the tumbler before it falls to the floor.

AMANDA	Father, she has fainted.
JOHN	Yes, our glass might have been broken.
SARA	Amanda, help me with her. We must lay her on my bed for a while. She needs a rest.
JOHN	Yes, it will do her good.

Amanda and Sara support Amelia out left. John looks at his watch.

It will not be long now. (*He sinks into a chair and buries his head in his hands.*)

Enter Amanda.

AMANDA   Father, Father, do not be unhappy, Father. (*She puts her arm round John.*) Does it not make you happy, Father, that we have given food and shelter to that poor girl in there?

JOHN   You are right, Amanda, it does make me happy that we have done some good.

Enter Sara.

SARA   She is sleeping peacefully now.

JOHN   It will be a pity to wake her at midnight, when the bailiffs come.

AMANDA   Perhaps if we told the bailiffs she is seriously ill, they would go away.

JOHN   No, Amanda, they are hard-hearted men.

A knock at the door. Amanda and Sara cling to one another. John stares in front of him.

AMANDA   Oh, Mother, Mother, what'll we do, Mother?

John takes out his watch.

SARA   The time, John, what is the time?

John shakes the watch violently.

JOHN   It's the same time as when I last looked at it.

SARA   Perhaps it has stopped, John.

John listens for the tick.

JOHN	Yes, Sara, it has never been the same since Amanda dropped it down the well.
AMANDA	Well, Father, you did say it was shockproof.

The knock is repeated, louder this time.

SARA	The door, John, open the door.
JOHN	Oh, yes, I had forgotten.

He stands and goes to the door. He opens it. A heavily cloaked figure staggers into the room. He carries a heavy sack which he dumps on the floor. His wide-brimmed hat, a large moustache and the collar of his cloak hide most of his features.

Come in, sir.

STRANGER	I am already in.
JOHN	You are tired, sir.
SARA	You appear to be exhausted, sir.
STRANGER	I have travelled far.
AMANDA	How far?
STRANGER	Too far.
AMANDA	How far is that?
STRANGER	Far enough.
AMANDA	But . . .
SARA	Quiet, Amanda!
STRANGER	I am weary. Every bone in my body aches. (*As he talks he lifts the sack and places it as a pillow on the bed.*) I can hardly keep my eyes open. My arms are hanging out of their sockets. My knees are knocking together with fatigue. (*He stretches out on the bed with his feet facing the audience.*) Ah, that's better! I feel like an angel on a cloud of down. Ah-h-h, yes, that's better! Like an angel on a cloud of down. (*His hat*

tips forward over his face as his head touches the sack.)
Ah-h-h!

A fairly long pause as the family gaze at their slumbering visitor.

AMANDA   He doesn't look like an angel.

The stranger snores loudly.

He doesn't sound like one either.

SARA   But, John, what are we going to do with him? We can't just leave him there.

JOHN   It doesn't matter, Sara, he might as well have a few moments' rest. He will be shifted when the bailiffs come.

AMANDA   But who is he, Father, who is he?

JOHN   I don't know, Amanda.

AMANDA   And I wonder what he's got in that sack. I know, Father, I know who he is!

JOHN   Who is he, Amanda?

AMANDA   He's Father Christmas.

SARA   Oh, no!

AMANDA   But he is, Mother. Father Christmas always has a sack of toys for good little girls.

JOHN   You can hardly be described as a little girl, Amanda.

SARA   And you're certainly not good.

Amanda flings herself weeping into a chair. Sara follows her daughter and puts her arm round her.

There, there, my poor baby. Mummy's sorry. Mummy didn't really mean it. There, there.

A knock at the door. The family look at one another.

This *will* be the bailiffs.

AMANDA   Oh, Mother!

John strides to the door.

JOHN   Well, we might as well get it over with.

Sara and Amanda stand huddled together.

SARA   We must try to be brave.

John opens the door. Adolphus walks in. He is dressed as a convict. Arms are flung wide as they greet one another.

ADOLPHUS Father!

JOHN   Adolphus!

ADOLPHUS Sister!

AMANDA   Brother!

ADOLPHUS Mother!

SARA   Son!

Adolphus and Sara embrace.

My son, my son. My little boy! My Adolphus!

JOHN   But, Adolphus, how did you get away?

ADOLPHUS It was difficult, Father, but I made it. It was a bit of a job, persuading the warders to let me go, but they saw my point when I showed them this. (*He produces a wicked-looking knife.*)

AMANDA   Did someone give it to you for Christmas, Adolphus?

ADOLPHUS No, Amanda, I found it in the governor's house when I was decorating his Christmas tree.

JOHN   But they will come for you, Adolphus; they will take you back.

ADOLPHUS Never mind that, Father; at least I will have Christmas at home. The bloodhounds never work on Christmas Day.

SARA	Do sit down, my son.
ADOLPHUS	Thanks, Mother. (*He sits.*) Ah, it's good to be home. But where are the decorations and the Christmas tree?
SARA	My son, you have come home at a very unhappy time. There will be no Christmas for us.
ADOLPHUS	No Christmas! You mean there's no turkey in the larder, no plum pudding, no crackers?
AMANDA	There is no nothing, Adolphus.
JOHN	No *anything*, Amanda.
AMANDA	No anything, then, but it's not going to make much difference to my stomach.
ADOLPHUS	You mean it will be a waste of time hanging up my Christmas stocking?
SARA	My dear boy, there will not even be a bed on which to hang your stocking.
JOHN	There will be no bedroom.
AMANDA	There will be no home.
ADOLPHUS	No stocking, no bed, no home! But, Mother, this is our home.
SARA	No, Adolphus, at midnight this will no longer be our home.
ADOLPHUS	Oh, no!
AMANDA	Oh, yes!
SARA	It is a sad story, my son. You see, our home is mortgaged, and we owe five hundred pounds to the Farmstead Development Company.
JOHN	At midnight the bailiffs will come. I have tried hard, but I cannot find five hundred pounds.
ADOLPHUS	But couldn't you borrow five hundred pounds, Father?

AMANDA	Oh, don't be silly, Adolphus. Everyone knows Father too well to lend him money.
SARA	Amanda, don't be cheeky.
ADOLPHUS	I see, I see. So you need five hundred pounds and you need it in a hurry.

There is a loud snore from the bed.

	But, mother, who's that? Who's that on the bed?
SARA	He's a weary traveller, my son. He arrived only a short time ago. He looked so tired that we decided to lend him the bed for a while.

Adolphus creeps across to the bed and peeps at the sleeper. He does not, however, lift the brim of the hat.

ADOLPHUS	(*eagerly*) Father, was he carrying a sack, a heavy sack?
JOHN	That's right, son.
AMANDA	Yes, that's right. Look, he's using it as a pillow.
ADOLPHUS	Father, do you know what's in the sack?
JOHN	No, son, I haven't the faintest idea.
AMANDA	Is it food, Adolphus, is it food?
ADOLPHUS	There is a million pounds in banknotes in that sack.
JOHN/SARA/ AMANDA	A million pounds!
SARA	But, Adolphus, how do you know?
ADOLPHUS	I watched him count them. You see, I was hiding in a bush and he sat down nearly beside me to count the money. When he resumed his journey I followed him for a while. Then I saw a policeman and had to hide. When I came out of hiding he had gone.
AMANDA	A million pounds. Think of all the ice-lollies you could buy with a million pounds.

| ADOLPHUS | Father, you need five hundred pounds. This man has a million. Father, is there a poker handy? |
| SARA | Oh, my son, my son! I knew you would save us. I knew you would think of something. |

John fetches the poker. It is a very large, ugly weapon.

| JOHN | I have it here. It's good and solid. We bought it before the war. (*He pats his son on the back.*) My boy, I am proud of you. I always knew you had brains. |

John reaches the head of the bed. He raises the poker ready to strike.

| AMANDA | Don't miss, Father. |
| ADOLPHUS | No, Father, give it to me. I will do it. |

John lowers the weapon.

| JOHN | Of course, son, you have had more experience. I am just a selfish old man. (*He gives Adolphus the poker.*) |
| ADOLPHUS | Thanks, Dad. |

Adolphus takes careful aim and raises the poker above the head of the sleeper. He is just about to strike when . . .

AMANDA	Would it not be better on the point of the jaw, Adolphus.
ADOLPHUS	Amanda, please, how can I concentrate?
SARA	Quiet, Amanda. Adolphus knows best. Adolphus is an expert.

Adolphus again raises the poker. Again he is about to strike . . .

| AMANDA | Wouldn't it be easier if you took his hat off, Adolphus? |
| ADOLPHUS | My dear sister, I know what I'm doing. Now will you please keep quiet while I get on with the job. |

| AMANDA | Well, I was only trying to help. |
| ADOLPHUS | Now, then. |

Again he raises the poker. He is just about to strike when the bells of Christmas Day ring out. They all listen for a moment. Then Sara rushes forward and holds Adolphus' poker-arm.

| SARA | No, Adolphus, no! It is Christmas Day. Not on Christmas Day. Can you not hear the Christmas bells ringing out their message of goodwill? |
| JOHN | I'm afraid your mother is right, son. It is the day of goodwill. Strike no blow on Christmas Day. Couldn't we leave it till tomorrow? Listen to the bells, my boy. Do they not fill your heart with love for your fellow man? |

Suddenly Richard sits bolt upright on the bed. The hat falls from his face.

| RICHARD | Those bells, those bells! Just listen to those bells. I must be in heaven. Perhaps I am an angel after all. |
| AMANDA | You very nearly were, sir. |

Up to now Richard has been gazing straight at the audience. When he hears Amanda's voice he looks round at the assembled family.

| SARA | My son, my son, Richard! |

Each of the characters flings his or her arms wide at the greeting.

RICHARD	Mother!
JOHN	Son!
RICHARD	Father!
ADOLPHUS	Brother!

RICHARD	Brother!
AMANDA	My other brother!
RICHARD	Sister!
SARA	Oh, my darling boy, my Richard! (*She embraces him.*)
AMANDA	And to think we nearly crowned him with a poker.

Richard lifts the sack and holds it head high.

RICHARD	I did it, Mother, I did it! I made a million pounds. And here it is in the sack.
JOHN	You are indeed welcome, Richard. I always knew you had it in you.
RICHARD	But, Adolphus, what are you doing here in this outfit? Have you been in jail?
ADOLPHUS	Yes, Richard, I have. But I managed to slip away for Christmas.
RICHARD	Good, this is going to be a happy family reunion.
AMANDA	Ah, but they haven't told you about the mortgage, Richard.
RICHARD	What mortgage?
AMANDA	Father took out a mortgage on the farm, and we are going to be turned out at midnight because he cannot pay the money back. He owes five hundred pounds to the Farmstead Development Company.
RICHARD	Did you say the Farmstead Development Company?
AMANDA	Yes, that's right, Father, isn't it?
JOHN	That's right, daughter.
RICHARD	But I own the Farmstead Development Company.
ALL	What!
RICHARD	Yes, I own it. That's how I made my million pounds. And now, now, I can see what a swine I have been, making money out of poor, wretched folks like

yourselves. To think I've been robbing my own dear family! Mother, can you ever forgive me?

SARA Don't be sad, Richard, of course I forgive you. After all, you have brought it back to us in the sack, haven't you?

AMANDA Yes, but only just in time.

RICHARD Oh, my conscience, my conscience! How can I make amends for all the wrong I have done? I had not realised it before, sitting at my desk in my office in the big city. Oh, Mother, what can I do to undo all the wrong I have done?

AMANDA You could give it all back.

JOHN Don't be ridiculous, Amanda. After all, I'm sure Richard can't remember all the names of the people he has robbed.

RICHARD Yes, it would be difficult to remember all those names, but perhaps if I tried hard . . .

ADOLPHUS I shouldn't try too hard, Richard.

SARA Adolphus is right, Richard, you must not distress your poor tired brain.

Amelia enters and stands in the doorway.

RICHARD No, I won't try too hard.

Adolphus sees Amelia and flings his arms wide.

ADOLPHUS Amelia!

Amelia does the same.

AMELIA Adolphus!

They embrace.

SARA You two know each other?

ADOLPHUS She's my wife.

AMELIA	He's my husband.
AMANDA	What a strange coincidence.

Sara flings her arms wide.

SARA	Daughter-in-law!

Amelia does the same.

AMELIA	Mother-in-law!
JOHN	But, son, we didn't even know you were married.
ADOLPHUS	I meant to tell you, but I never got round to it.
SARA	Never mind that, John. Think of what a happy Christmas we're going to have.
JOHN	Yes, my dear, with all our family around us.
AMANDA	And hardly a thing to eat in the house.
SARA	You forget, dear daughter, Richard has a sack full of money.
AMANDA	You forget, dear Mother, none of the shops is open on Christmas Day.

Quick curtain.

Losing Paradise

David Calcutt

List of Characters

Adam
Eve

Eve is onstage. Adam enters.

ADAM Quick! He's coming –

EVE What?

ADAM He's coming, here –

EVE Who?

ADAM Who do you think?

EVE Him?

ADAM Yes!

EVE Here?

ADAM Yes! Here! We've got to go, get out, quick –

EVE Get out –

ADAM Hide.

EVE Hide –

ADAM That's what I said! Stop repeating everything! There's no time. Get your shoes on. Come on! Hurry! He'll be here any minute!

EVE How do you know? How do you know he's coming here?

ADAM I know.

EVE Why is he coming? What does he want?

ADAM Can't you guess? There's only one reason. Only one reason why he'd be coming here.

EVE He knows –

ADAM That's right –

EVE	He knows about us – what we –
ADAM	You've got it.
EVE	He found out.
ADAM	He must have done.
EVE	Or somebody told him.
ADAM	Maybe –
EVE	Somebody told him –
ADAM	Have you got them on?
EVE	What?
ADAM	Your shoes –
EVE	My shoes –
ADAM	Get them on.
EVE	I don't care about my shoes! What does it matter if I've got my shoes on or not? It doesn't matter about my shoes! Somebody told him!
ADAM	I don't know –
EVE	They must have done.
ADAM	Not necessarily –
EVE	How else would he know unless somebody told him? Somebody.
ADAM	Me? You mean me? You're saying I told him? You think that I told him? Me? You're saying me?
EVE	Who else? Who else is there that knows? There's nobody else. Nobody else knows. Only us. And now him. Now he knows. So who told him? Tell me that! Go on! Tell me! You tell me who told him!
ADAM	Not me.
EVE	Who, then? Who else? Who? Me? You think that it was me?
ADAM	You think that it was me –
EVE	I know that it was you.

ADAM You know?

EVE I know.

ADAM Oh, that's sweet, that is. That's sweet, coming from you. Very sweet. I can see you, now. Oh, yes. I see what you really are. I can see right through. Under the skin. Right under. Where the bone is. Where the gristle is. Where the worms are. I can see the worms wriggling under your skin.

EVE You see that, do you?

ADAM I see all that.

EVE Shall I tell you what I see?

ADAM Go on, then. Tell me.

EVE I see deeper. I see under the gristle, under the bones. I see through the space between the bones. I see all the way down to the cellar. I see the cellar door. I see what's behind the door. I see what's hidden deep down in the cellar.

ADAM We'd better go.

EVE Where? Where shall we go? Where can we go?

ADAM I don't know. Somewhere. Anywhere. Away.

EVE Why not stay?

ADAM Stay?

EVE Stay. Stay and hide.

ADAM Hide? Where? Where shall we hide? Where can we hide?

EVE I don't know. Somewhere. Anywhere. Stand still. Stand very still. Stand completely still. Hold your breath. Don't blink. Look straight ahead. Maybe he won't notice us. Maybe he'll think we're just part of the furniture.

ADAM It won't work. He'll see us. He'll know it's us. He knows us. He'll find us. No matter how we stand. No matter where we hide. He'll sniff us out.

EVE	Fee Fi Fo Fum.
ADAM	Grind our bones.
EVE	To make his bread.
ADAM	We'd better go. Now.
EVE	Wait. Let me get my shoes on.
ADAM	Your shoes – ?
EVE	It won't take long –
ADAM	I thought you'd done that –
EVE	No – I'm doing it now –
ADAM	Hurry up –
EVE	Almost done –
ADAM	Come on –
EVE	It's done! They're on!
ADAM	Let's run!
EVE	Did you hear something? Did you hear something just then?
ADAM	I'm not sure –
EVE	A noise –
ADAM	A sound –
EVE	Did you? Just then?
ADAM	Yes – yes – just then – and again!
EVE	Again!
ADAM	It came from outside.
EVE	Outside the door.
ADAM	Someone's outside.
EVE	Someone's outside the door.
ADAM	Knocking.
EVE	Someone's knocking at the door.
ADAM	It's like that dream, that you have at night.

EVE	When you hear that sound and it gives you a fright.
ADAM	That booming sound –
EVE	Like waves on the shore.
ADAM	That sound of the thunder.
EVE	That knocking on the door.
ADAM	He wants to come in.
EVE	Don't let him in.
ADAM	He wants to come in.
EVE	Don't – don't let him in.
ADAM	Is this a bad dream?
EVE	This is no dream.
ADAM	Will we wake up soon?
EVE	We're already awake.
ADAM	He's knocking at the door.
EVE	We won't let him in.
ADAM	He wants to come in.
EVE	Don't – don't – don't let him in.

They cower together in the corner.

It's a Kind of Magic!

Steven Deproost

List of Characters

Ali
Chorus
Ray
Mrs Grimm
Mum
Showman 1
Showman 2
Bank manager
Headmistress

NOTES

Showmen can be male or female.

ALI	It was the end of the summer holidays. Everyone was getting bored, hanging about outside . . .
ONE CHORUS VOICE	. . . in the heat . . .
ONE CHORUS VOICE	. . . getting sweaty and thirsty . . .
ONE CHORUS VOICE	. . . winding each other up . . .
ALI	. . . calling each other names.
ONE CHORUS VOICE	Someone ends up getting picked on.
RAY	Yea, someone like me.
CHORUS	A-a-h. Poor Raymond. Poor Raymondo.
ONE CHORUS VOICE	Hey, Ray.
ONE CHORUS VOICE	What you doing today, Ray?
ONE CHORUS VOICE	Got anything to say, Ray?
ONE CHORUS VOICE	Come on, Ray, ain't you going to play, Ray?
ONE CHORUS VOICE	Are you gay, Ray?

ONE CHORUS VOICE	Don't run away, Ray.
ONE CHORUS VOICE	Stay, Ray.
ONE CHORUS VOICE	It's a pity your family isn't called Gunn – Ray Gunn.
CHORUS	Ha, ha, ha.
ONE CHORUS VOICE	Are you Mummy's little ray of sunshine?
ONE CHORUS VOICE	Does the sun shine out of your arse?
ALI	I think we'd better stop this here, before they switch us off. Enter Mrs Grimm.
MRS GRIMM	I've had enough of you lot hanging about. Haven't you got homes of your own? I told you yesterday not to sit on that fence.
ONE CHORUS VOICE	What are fences for?
MRS GRIMM	What did you say?
ONE CHORUS VOICE	I was just telling her to put her feet on the floor.
MRS GRIMM	Haven't you got anything better to do? When I was your age . . .
ONE CHORUS VOICE	I was working down a mine.
MRS GRIMM	What did you say?
ONE CHORUS VOICE	You knew what to do with your time.
MRS GRIMM	Exactly. I'm glad one of you's got some sense. I remember an afternoon like this in the summer of 1944 – of course it was still the war then . . .
CHORUS	We're going. Goodbye, Mrs Grimm.
ONE CHORUS VOICE	Back indoors. Sitting alone.
ONE CHORUS VOICE	Games on the PC.
ONE CHORUS VOICE	Music on the CD.
ONE CHORUS VOICE	Quiz shows on the TV.
ONE CHORUS VOICE	Chatting on the mobile phone.

	Build up an appropriate soundscape which continues under the following:
ONE CHORUS VOICE	Everyone is so busy with electronic entertainment
ONE CHORUS VOICE	beamed in from far and wide
ONE CHORUS VOICE	they fail to notice the electrical excitement
ONE CHORUS VOICE	which is gathering outside.
ALI	Then suddenly . . .

The soundscape dies and there is a tremendous crack of thunder.

ONE CHORUS VOICE	It cricked and cracked.
ONE CHORUS VOICE	It flicked and flacked.
ONE CHORUS VOICE	It shicked and shacked.
ONE CHORUS VOICE	It poured.

More lightning, thunder and heavy rain.

ONE CHORUS VOICE	Mum, it's gone dark. (*repeated switching*)
ONE CHORUS VOICE	Mum, the screen's gone blank. (*tapping keyboard*)
ONE CHORUS VOICE	What's happened to my music?
MUM	The electricity's off.
ALI	Aww!
MUM	I'm sure they'll fix it soon.
ALI	But an hour passes in that room And still they sit there in the gloom.
ONE CHORUS VOICE	They stare out through the window into the night.
ONE CHORUS VOICE	They wait for those flashes that put dark to flight.

ONE CHORUS VOICE	The lights stay off. The house is dead.
ONE CHORUS VOICE	And so at last they go to bed.

*Exterior. Storm. Storm subsides. Bright morning
birdsong. A rhythm can be heard in the distance.
The showmen are approaching. Fade to interior.*

ONE CHORUS VOICE	(*yawning*) Morning!
ONE CHORUS VOICE	(*yawning*) Morning!
BOTH	What a night!
ONE CHORUS VOICE	What's that? Listen!
ONE CHORUS VOICE	I can't hear anything – still no television, no radio, no music, no dishwasher, no washing machine, no kettle, no toaster, no shower . . .
ONE CHORUS VOICE	S-sh! There *is* something. Open the window.
ONE CHORUS VOICE	What is it?
ONE CHORUS VOICE	I don't know. Get dressed, we're going to find out!
CHORUS	Within an hour Of this dawn without power Everyone has heard the beat Everyone is on their feet They put on T-shirts, socks and trousers Grab their shoes and leave their houses And venture out into the street.
ONE CHORUS VOICE	Did you see the lightning?
ONE CHORUS VOICE	Did you hear the thunder?
ONE CHORUS VOICE	Have you ever seen such rain?
ONE CHORUS VOICE	If we lived to be a hundred and three, we might never see that again.
ONE CHORUS VOICE	Where's everyone going?
ONE CHORUS VOICE	What's all the fuss?

ONE CHORUS VOICE	I don't know.
ONE CHORUS VOICE	I haven't a clue.
ONE CHORUS VOICE	Just follow the beat.
ONE CHORUS VOICE	Dance down the street.
ONE CHORUS VOICE	That's all you need to do.

Rhythm/music comes to a climax.

CHORUS	Come on down Something's going on in town.
SHOWMAN 1	Ladies and gentlemen
SHOWMAN 2	boys and girls
SHOWMAN 1	we present to you
SHOWMAN 2	for one day only
SHOWMAN 1	a once-in-a-life-time experience
SHOWMAN 2	amazing feats of acrobatic artistry
SHOWMAN 1	cacophonous, rib-cracking comedy
SHOWMAN 1 AND 2	(*alternately*) the strongest . . . the bravest . . . the shortest . . . the tallest . . . the fattest . . . the thinnest . . . the meanest . . . the greenest . . . the most melancholy . . . the most hilarious . . . the cleverest . . . the craziest . . .

Drum roll/cymbal.

The Greatest Show on Earth!

SHOWMAN 1	You're all very quiet. Have we made ourselves clear?
SHOWMAN 2	It's champion to see so many of you here.
SHOWMAN 1	Young man/woman at the back –
ONE CHORUS VOICE	What time is the show?
SHOWMAN 1	Three o'clock, as far as I know.
ONE CHORUS VOICE	And where will it be?

SHOWMAN 2	Right on this spot.
MRS GRIMM	Whether the council likes it or not?
SHOWMAN 2	Mrs Grimm, have no fear. All of your councillors are with us out here.
SHOWMAN 1	And if they want to keep their positions They'll give us the requisite permissions.
SHOWMAN 2	Now we need every child, woman and man to put up the big top and empty the van.
ALI	So all together we emptied the load and up went the big top right across the main road.
SHOWMAN 1 AND 2	After three . . . 1 . . . 2 . . . 3 . . .
CHORUS	He-e-ave . . . He-e-ave . . . He-e-ave . . . Hurray! Unfolding and threading and stitching and stretching Pulling and pushing and carrying and fetching Bolting and banging and so it went on Till at ten to three the job was done.
SHOWMAN 1	Take your seats, ladies and gentlemen!
ONE CHORUS VOICE	Why haven't they taken any money off us?
SHOWMAN 2	Hurry along there, please, boys and girls. The show's about to begin.
ONE CHORUS VOICE	Where are all the performers?
SHOWMAN 1	*Fanfare.* And now, my friends, the moment you have all been waiting for . . . *Fanfare.*
SHOWMAN 2	Just a minute. We don't *know* what they've been waiting for.
SHOWMAN 1	By Jove! You're right. We'd better ask.

SHOWMAN 2	Sir, be so kind as to tell us what you are waiting for?
ONE CHORUS VOICE	The electricity to come back on.
SHOWMAN 2	There's always one, isn't there?
SHOWMAN 1	How about you, madam?
MRS GRIMM	I always used to like the clowns. I haven't had a good laugh in years. I remember a circus in the summer of 1947 . . .
SHOWMAN 1	Thank you, Mrs Grimm. Anyone else waiting for the clowns?
	A selection of 'Me, me!'s.
SHOWMAN 2	Our first act today, dear patrons, all the way from here, there and everywhere . . .
SHOWMAN 1	. . . but especially from here . . .
SHOWMAN 2	. . . those harbingers of hilarity . . .
SHOWMAN 1 AND 2	. . . introducing . . . (*alternately*) Mrs Grimm . . . Ali . . . Sarah . . .
ALI	(*whispering aside*) How do they know our names?
SHOWMAN 1 AND 2	. . . Mark, Josh, Zia and Nareen . . .
	Fanfare.
SHOWMAN 1	Yes, put your hands together for –
SHOWMAN 1 AND 2	Mrs Grimm and the Grimmettes!
	Silence.
ALI	There was a stunned silence. Then it began, just like the rain had the night before . . .
	Isolated clapping which builds gradually to wild applause and cheering.

We walked into the arena and somehow as if by magic we did it.

Laughter.

So the show went on.

More laughter.

ONE CHORUS VOICE	The Great Raymondo amazed us with his antics on the fairly-high-wire.

Gasping and clapping from the crowd.

ONE CHORUS VOICE	The bank manager mystified us with magic:
BANK MANAGER	Here's a pound in your pocket . . . Now you see it . . . Now you don't.
ONE CHORUS VOICE	The headmistress astounded us with the bravery of her toddler-taming act:
HEADMISTRESS	(*with roaring and whip-cracking*) Back! Back! Lie-down!
ALI	The show went on and on till everyone had taken part
ONE CHORUS VOICE	Even if their contribution was just a well-timed fart
ALI	Till finally at half-past ten
ONE CHORUS VOICE	Drunk with laughter
ALI	We staggered home again.
ONE CHORUS VOICE	What a day!
ALI	We let ourselves in through the still-dark door And felt our way into bed once more.
ONE CHORUS VOICE	Good night.
ONE CHORUS VOICE	Sleep tight.
BOTH	What a day!

Repeat of dawn sounds. Birdsong. But this time gradually drowned out by noise of traffic and electrical gadgets.

ALI	Next morning we ran into town, first thing.
ONE CHORUS VOICE	To help take the big top down.
ALI	But everything was gone.
ONE CHORUS VOICE	Except the traffic and the shopping and . . .
ALI	It was as if nothing had really happened.
ONE CHORUS VOICE	The grown-ups didn't talk about it.
ALI	As if each one thought it had been their own private dream.
ONE CHORUS VOICE	No one dared write anything in the paper.
ALI	But we know. Don't we?
ONE CHORUS VOICE	Mrs Grimm has a twinkle in her eye that was never there before.
ONE CHORUS VOICE	You can occasionally catch the headteacher skipping down the corridor.
ONE CHORUS VOICE	No one ever says they don't know what to do.
ALI	And sometimes, if you're awake at dawn, you can open the window, you can just hear that beat, somewhere in the distance.

The rhythm is heard faintly.

Activities

Say Yes!

By Steven Deproost

Speaking and Listening

1 *Say Yes!* is a radio script. In groups of six, read the script and plan
   a radio performance. First talk about the different voices needed to
   make the play effective; then plan what music and sound effects
   you will need. Then record it. Listen to the recording, decide on
   which parts you want to improve and then record a final version.

2 The play is an attack on the 'consumer society' – a world in which
   we are constantly being pressured to buy new things whether we
   need them or not. Talk about the times when you (or someone you
   know) might have bought something because of the label, or
   because everybody else had one. Then discuss the ways in which
   the script attacks the consumer society and the way advertisers try
   to get us to buy more and more products.

Reading

Reread *Say Yes!* and make a note on all the features which show that
it is a radio script rather than a stage or screen script. For example,
which actions or sections of dialogue are difficult to perform on stage,
but can sound effective on radio?

Writing

Make a copy of the leaflet that Laura and her friends have produced.
Decide exactly what it would say about shopping, advertising and the
consumer society. Invent some anti-consumer jingles in the same
style as the jingles chanted by the chorus on pages 12–13.

Get 'Em

By Farrukh Dhondy

Speaking and Listening

1   As a class, talk about your experience of video games. Why are they popular, would you say? What percentage of them involve violence of one kind or another? Why are violent games so attractive? Are they equally popular with girls and boys?

2   When you have read the play, talk about the characters' names. What do the names tell you about what these characters represent? (Try putting pairs of names together and see what you end up with.)

Reading

Read through the script again and make notes in the form of a diagram to show what happens in the room and on the screen. For example, make a note of the different points at which Kay and Oss are no longer on screen, but are part of the real world.

Writing

1   Write a section of a play in which somebody interacts with a video game. Try to make it different from *Get 'Em* by including a completely different kind of game in your script: one that does not involve violence.

2   Write the script for the scene which takes place when Reception turns the game on again and Kay starts playing. Which new characters are now on screen? Invent names for them. What kind of game do they start playing with Kay? How does it end?

The Mobile

By Mark Morris

Speaking and Listening

In groups of three, plan a performance of *The Mobile*. There isn't much action in the play, so think about the ways in which you will make the three characters different and interesting. Then rehearse the script, trying to make the tongue-twisting word-play (' . . . he hates Kaz coz Kaz is my cuz . . . ') as fast and witty as possible.

Reading

When he wrote this play, Mark Morris had to think up all the abbreviated words he could which formed a particular pattern. He started with the characters, Baz, Daz and Gaz. Reread the script and note down all the words which are part of the same pattern. Next to each one, write the longer word that it comes from. Start off with *Baz – Barry*.

Writing

Write a script for a telephone call between two characters called Jo and Mo. Try to include some word-play like Mark Morris's.

Windfalls

By Steven Deproost

Speaking and Listening

1   A stereotype is a fixed image that people have in their minds of a particular type of person. For example, for many years the stereotype 'baddie' in a western always had a black hat and a thin moustache. What is the stereotype of 'an old person'? What do old people look like? How do they move? What things are they interested in? What do they typically talk about? List examples of stereotypes of old people on television. Then think about Flora. What shows that Max believes that Flora will be a stereotypical 'old person'? What proves that she isn't?

2   What would be the best way to stage *Windfalls*? Talk about the set and the props that would be needed for a stage production.

Reading

Unlike a novel, where the narrator can provide us with all sorts of important details, a play has to rely on the dialogue and stage directions to get information across. Find the information in the dialogue which helps us to answer the following questions:

1   Who is Max?
2   Where has he come from?
3   What are his aims as he approaches Flora?
4   When do we realise that the tables have been turned on Max? How does the dramatist neatly get that fact across to us?

Writing

Write either:

1   the glossy leaflet produced by Max's company; or
2   the letter that Flora writes to a friend in which she encloses the leaflet and recounts the incident with Max.

The Bully

By Gene Kemp

Speaking and Listening

In groups, improvise an incident of bullying. Afterwards, talk about what you have learned by acting the incident out. Has it helped you to understand what triggers an incident of bullying, for example? Could it have been avoided? What made the bullies act as they did? Talk about the ways forward, after this incident has taken place. What could happen to stop the bully from bullying anyone else, and the victim from being bullied again?

Reading

Scenes 1 and 13 take place in the present day, when the narrator is a young office-worker. All the scenes in between are a flash-back to twelve years earlier. In pairs, discuss whether, in your opinion, the play as a whole has a happy ending or a sad one (or a mixture of the two). Back up your impression with evidence from the play. (In particular, what does the description of the bully Houseman in Scene 13 make you feel?)

Writing

Write a short scene between Jim and Houseman ten years after their meeting at the bus stop. This time Jim actually speaks to Houseman. What is each one of them doing with his life by this time? What do they say to each other?

Witness

By Paul Francis

Speaking and Listening

What would you do in Marie's position? In groups of four, improvise conversations between **a**) Ben and Clare; and **b**) Marie and her mother, on the day the news comes through that Terry is pleading not guilty. What do Ben and Marie decide to do? What is Marie's mother's advice? From your reading of the play, and what you have learned about the characters, what do you think will happen?

Reading

One of the things that *Witness* shows us is that people often know very little about their friends or their relations. Reread the dialogue, and then in your groups discuss how much you think Marie's mother understands about Marie's friends and the situation involving Terry.

Writing

1   Write Mrs Colton's diary entry for the day on which the play ends. What does she say about the possibility of a court case? What will she advise Marie to do?

2   Suppose Terry decides to plead not guilty and the police come to question Marie. In pairs, improvise the conversation between the police and Marie, and then write the statement that Marie gives to the police.

Joyride

By Steve Barlow and Steve Skidmore

Speaking and Listening

1   By the end of the play, each of the characters probably has one or
two overriding thoughts or feelings. For example, the child's
mother would be grieving for her daughter and dreading having to
inform her husband. What is the main thought or feeling that each
of these characters has on their mind:

   a First youth;

   b Detective;

   c Mum;

   d Eyewitness?

   Talk about it in pairs. Then pick one line from each of these
characters' speeches and say it in a way that brings out this main
thought or feeling.

2   Experiment with different ways of saying the final line. What is the
Detective getting at? What feeling do you want to leave the
audience with?

3   In groups of six, create a freeze-frame of the moment in the final
scene when five of the characters all speak at almost the same
time. Think about the expression that each character should have
and work out an appropriate frozen action or gesture.

Reading

Joyride is made up of twelve very short scenes and there are obviously
gaps in time between, say, the first and second appearances of the
Police officer talking to the girl's mother, or the Eyewitness talking to
the Reporter. Reread the script and jot down what seems to have
happened between the first and second, and second and third,
appearances of:

1   Phil's two friends (First and Second youth);

2   Phil's parents.

Writing

Write a script for eight or nine short scenes which take place that night between: Phil and his parents; the Police officer and the Detective; the Eyewitness and a neighbour; and Phil's two friends (First and Second youth). Write in the same style as *Joyride*, keeping each scene very brief and interweaving the scenes, cutting from one conversation to the next. Remember that a little time will have passed between each pair's first and second scene.

Pressure Point

By Anthony Masters

Speaking and Listening

In small groups, talk about the three characters.

Why have Karl and Jason broken into Mrs Samuels's house (it's not just for what they can steal). What do you learn about them? Do you think that the excuse they give for their behaviour (to do with school, page 68) is reasonable? What reason does Karl give for claiming that they will never again break in anywhere (look at the final line of the play)? What exactly does he mean? Mrs Samuels is clearly a courageous woman. What makes her change her mind about phoning for the police?

Reading

Reread the play and note down everything which helps us to understand what drove the boys to commit the break-in. Then use the information to write a short scene which comes before the beginning of the play. You could include the dare that Jason talks about and perhaps some dialogue about the need to impress their girlfriends (page 64).

Writing

Although this is a story about a break-in, the real interest centres on the dialogue between Mrs Samuels and the boys. Pick a section of the play and redraft it as a radio play. Use the existing dialogue, but add extra dialogue if you need to in order to make clear what is going on. You should also include any sound effects that the listener will hear.

At the Post Office

By George Kulbacki and Di Timmins

Speaking and Listening

In pairs, make a list of the clues which told you what Bruce and Roger, in fact, were. When did you become sure? For example, was it the news that Max had been involved in a fight? Or that Mrs Williams had 'dragged him off home'?

Reading

In pairs, look back at the script and talk about all the things the writers have done to make us believe for as long as possible that the characters are human. For example, what is typically 'human' about the title of the sketch, or the opening dozen lines? List all the things that Bruce and Roger discuss which, at first sight, seem to be about human activities, but on closer reading turn out to be about something altogether different.

Writing

Write a scene between two pets (not dogs) in which they discuss life in their households. For example, what do neighbouring cats have to say to each other when they meet at the end of the garden? What would a pair of goldfish have to talk about, or gerbils? Write in a style similar to *At the Post Office*, so that a reader would not realise until some way through the sketch that the characters were pets.

Home *and* Spies

By Ken Campbell

Speaking and Listening

1   Some scripts are great fun to rehearse. In pairs, practise the sequence in *Spies* from the point where Keith suggests that they have to go 'Thppppp!' every time they mean what they say (pages 86–87). Then improvise a conversation of your own in which everything you say means the opposite unless you go 'Thppppp!' first.

2   Rehearse and perform either *Home* or *Spies* in front of an audience that has not read it. Afterwards hold a discussion and ask the audience for their responses. Who did they think the two men were? What did they think was the 'real' situation (if anything)? How easy did they find it to follow the twists and turns of the plot?

Reading

These two scripts are written without stage directions. Reread either *Home* or *Spies* and add stage directions (or director's notes) to help the actors perform the sketch and get the plot across clearly to the audience. For example, where are Johnstone and Keith, and what are they doing at the opening of *Home*? What does Keith do as he says 'I don't know' (page 78)? Read the dialogue carefully before you make any suggestions.

Writing

As each of these sketches unfolds, the characters in turn give us a different and new picture of 'reality'. For example, in *Home*, Keith reveals that he is the 'Evil Genius' (page 81), only for Johnstone to confess that he is actually a robot replica (page 81)! Write your own play with a similar framework, in which characters reveal amazing things about themselves and then deny them at the end.

The Off-side Trap

By Mary Colson

Speaking and Listening

1   In groups of four, talk about some of the difficulties you have experienced in meeting somebody new and trying to get the conversation going. What kind of thing did you say – and did it work?

2   Perform the script twice. First act it out with four actors (two playing Maxine and Paul, two others playing their thoughts). Then perform it with only the two characters, but making sure that the thoughts come across, even though they are not spoken. Discuss how doing the first version helped with the second.

Reading

Note down all the things we learn from the characters' thoughts which show **a**) that Maxine and Paul have misunderstood one another; and **b**) that they have real differences in outlook and interests. In your groups, discuss how much chance Maxine and Paul's relationship has of succeeding.

Writing

1   Write a different ending to the scene from the point where Paul says, 'Maybe we could um . . . go out some time – ' (page 96). For example, what might happen if he invited Maxine out to a football match, rather than a film?

2   Write a similar scene between two people who have very different interests, in which the characters' thoughts are part of the script.

Date

By Ann Cartwright

Speaking and Listening

Perform the script in pairs as a radio play, making sure that you show the difference between the two characters in the way they speak. What kind of voice should each one have? Do they speak quickly or slowly? Do they have different accents? Does one of them hesitate a lot?

Reading

Discuss the following questions in groups:

1 Why do you think Ann Cartwright has chosen to give us no introductory stage directions for this sketch, not telling us where the conversation takes place, for example?
2 Why are the speakers called 1 and 2, rather than by character names?
3 What do we learn about each of the speakers from the dialogue?
4 What does 1 learn about 2 towards the end which changes the way he or she responds?
5 When you read the script, did you feel that the speakers were male or female, or one of each (and why)?

Writing

Imagine that the date does not go very well, and 2 decides to write to a problem-page agony aunt. Write 2's letter (making sure that it sounds as much like 2 as possible), explaining what went wrong and asking for advice.

Bright Lights

By David Calcutt

Speaking and Listening

Here is an outline of the old folk-tale *Hansel and Gretel*, first published by the Brothers Grimm in the early nineteenth century:

> *A brother and sister, Hansel and Gretel, are abandoned in the forest by their parents, who are too poor to feed them. Near to starvation, they find a cottage made of bread, cakes and sugar. They are busily eating when an old woman comes out and invites them in. Although they are frightened and have doubts about the old woman, they accept her invitation. She turns out to be a witch who imprisons Hansel – with the intention of fattening him up and eating him – and forces Gretel to work for her. When the time comes to bake Hansel in the oven, Gretel tricks the witch into looking into the oven and pushes her in. The two take the witch's jewels and return home.*

In groups of four, talk about the parallels between *Hansel and Gretel* and *Bright Lights*. What are the most obvious differences? What is the 'message' of the play, and how do the differences between it and the original folk-tale help to get the message across?

Reading

A narrator in a play (here called the Storyteller) has a number of jobs. For example, narrators can tell us what is going on, explain that time has passed, or give their own comments on the characters and their actions. Reread the play and make a list of the things that this narrator does. Redraft the opening of the play, up to 'Want something?' (page 104), without a narrator. Then discuss the differences between the two versions. What does the Storyteller add, or enable the writer to do?

Writing

Write the outline of a play set in the modern world and based upon another folk-tale such as *Little Red Riding Hood* or *The Three Little Pigs*. As David Calcutt did in *Bright Lights*, work out a plot which has parallels with the folk-tale but with one crucial difference. You could also give your play a 'message'.

The Mortgage

By Chris Burgess

Speaking and Listening

In the nineteenth century there was a very popular kind of play known as a 'melodrama'. The typical melodrama had:

> *innocent and virtuous heroes and heroines, who were often 'poor but honest';*
> *merciless villains, who were often rich landlords or businessmen;*
> *overdone, exaggerated language;*
> *highly dramatic acting;*
> *frequent points where the characters spoke directly to the audience;*
> *a sensational story-line, often full of plotting and deception;*
> *music to accompany the emotional scenes.*

In groups, find examples of each of these features in *The Mortgage*. Then perform one scene from the play in typically melodramatic style, overdoing the acting. Give someone the job of adding dramatic and emotional music in the background!

Reading

Different kinds of play, or novel, or film are called 'genres'. For example, film genres include westerns, science-fiction and horror. You can usually identify a genre by its typical features (such as the features of melodrama, listed above). A play or film which mocks one of these genres by laughing at the typical features is called a 'parody'. How can you tell that *The Mortgage* is a parody? Look at the list of melodrama features above and talk about the way in which each one is mocked and laughed at in *The Mortgage*.

Writing

Pick a different genre and write down some of its typical features. (For example, if you choose westerns, you might include gun-fights, sheriffs, wagon-trains and villains in black hats.) Then write a scene from a parody, in which some of the features you have written down are included for comic effect.

Losing Paradise

By David Calcutt

Speaking and Listening

In pairs, act out the scene, doing your best to bring out:

1   the tension and fear that the two characters experience;
2   the way they become increasingly suspicious of each other and
    begin to argue;
3   their reactions to the sound from outside.

Notice the way the lines begin to pick up a regular rhythm towards the
end, helped by the occasional rhyme and repetition. Get this across in
your performance.

Reading

Read the story of Adam and Eve in the Bible (Genesis, chapters 1–3).
Then talk about the ways in which David Calcutt has used this story.
Where does the play take place? Who is knocking? Why are Adam and
Eve frightened? What will happen when they try to run or hide?

Writing

Imagine you are directing a production of *Losing Paradise*. Write notes
for the actors which will help them perform the play, explaining how
they should react at a number of selected moments and how they
should say particular lines. Add some notes to show how the play will
be staged. (Is there any scenery, for example, or is the stage
completely bare?)

It's a Kind of Magic!

By Steven Deproost

Speaking and Listening

In groups, talk about your reactions to *It's a Kind of Magic!* What do you think it was 'about'? Did it have a 'message' of any kind? What was there about it that made it special? Think about the title: what 'kind of magic' had actually taken place by the end of the play? How had the people been changed?

Reading

1 Reread the script and note the moments where the characters speak in rhyme. Think about the different effects that rhyme can have in a play of this kind. Find examples of where rhyme is used:

   a to show the gang's mockery of the victim Ray;
   b to get across the monotony of daily life dominated by technology;
   c to represent the sound and appearance of lightning;
   d to show the passage of time from evening to night.

   Find other moments where rhyme is used and talk about the effect that it has.

2 Make a note on all the features which show that *It's a Kind of Magic!* is a radio script rather than a stage or screen script. For example, which parts of the story are difficult (or even impossible) to perform on stage, but can sound very effective on radio?

Writing

Write a short radio play which uses rhyme for different effects, as this script does. You might choose to include a chorus of voices and base the story on a small part of your local neighbourhood where something special – or even 'magical' – happens. Remember that things can happen in a radio play which would be impossible to show on stage and would require very expensive special effects in a film.

About the Authors

Steven Deproost

Steven studied medicine at university but eventually decided he was less likely to kill people if he worked in theatre. He trained as an actor at the Bristol Old Vic Theatre School and later took an MA in Playwriting Studies run by playwright David Edgar at Birmingham University. His acting experience includes film, television and radio but is mainly in theatre – especially community touring and theatre-in-education. In recent years he has done much more writing and he also runs projects based on writing and performance with schools and community groups. His current obsession is getting groups to create and record radio drama and other radio programmes. He works from his home in Stroud, Gloucestershire, where he lives with his partner and his son Theo, who is at the local junior school. His grown-up daughter Laura is working and sharing a flat in London. Sadly, Betty the family rat is now dead – but at least the telephone is more likely to stay connected.

Farrukh Dhondy

Farrukh was born in India and went to school there. He came to England to go to Cambridge University in the 1960s and began writing while he was at university. When he left university he did various odd jobs – washing up, painting houses, driving delivery vans – before becoming a teacher. He taught in inner London schools for ten years. At the time he belonged to small agitational political groups, mostly to do with 'immigrant' or black politics, and as part of their activities wrote in radical newspapers. An editor in a London publishing house read several of his pieces and asked Farrukh to write a book of stories. He couldn't believe his luck and so in 1976 his first book of short stories, called *East End at Your Feet* (Macmillan), was published. In the following years he wrote several books, among them *Trip Trap, Poona Company* and *Come to Mecca*. He left teaching in the late 1970s and began to write for TV and for the stage. He worked as a commissioning editor at Channel 4 for twelve years and then gave up full-time work to write again. He writes books, for adults and children, scripts for films and TV, and does some journalism.

Mark Morris

As well as running a successful English faculty in a Nottingham school, Mark Morris has produced a wide range of educational materials for classroom use. He has written textbooks, revision materials and spelling schemes. He has edited Shakespeare plays, adapted classic novels into more accessible formats, written original plays, edited dictionaries and even produced books of football trivia! He has also worked in a hamburger restaurant, a jewellery shop, a hospital, Alton Towers and Wembley Stadium as well as being a youth worker and a drugs counsellor.

He lives in a small Derbyshire village with his wife, son and two cats. He enjoys reading, all sorts of sport and avoiding doing the garden. He is also a fanatical Stoke City supporter, but is now happily getting therapy for this condition.

Gene Kemp

The very first story Gene wrote was for school assembly, and was entitled 'Toothie and Cat'. The students liked it and it went into a collection called *Dog Days and Cat Naps* (Faber and Faber). Later it was read on radio by Willie Rushton and Helen Mirren. After that Gene wrote many stories – first the *Tamworth Pig* stories and then the *Cricklepit School* stories, including the award-winning *The Turbulent Term of Tyke Tyler*, *Gowie Corby Plays Chicken*, and *Charlie Lewis Plays For Time* (Faber and Puffin). These stories have been translated into several languages, including Japanese and Afrikaans. 'Tyke' has been televised and there is also a drama version published by Oxford University Press and a musical 'Tyke' with music and lyrics by Allan Fouracre. Gene has also written an epic poem, *The Mink War*, which has been adapted for the stage, and *Mr Magus Is Waiting for You*, which was commissioned by the BBC. She wrote *The Bully* in collaboration with her son, who provided the necessary authenticity. Her latest book, *Bluebeard's Castle*, was published by Faber in 2000 – it is a humorous and satirical horror story for children.

Paul Francis

Paul Francis used to be a teacher and now works full-time as a writer. He is the author of the novel *Love and Chalkdust* (Liberty Books), and has written three collections of plays, including *Looking for the Moon* (CUP). He writes his own poetry, which he has performed at schools and at poetry festivals. In 2000 he won the Drama Association of Wales playwriting award, and the OUSS 'Sonnet at the Millennium' competition. With Gill Murray, he has edited two anthologies, on *Myths and Legends* and *Survivors* (Longman). He is producing an anthology of diaries and letters (Wordsworth), and writing a series of citizens' scripts. He lives in Much Wenlock, Shropshire, where he writes, reads, goes for walks and takes photographs.

Steve Barlow and Steve Skidmore

Steve Barlow and Steve Skidmore are both experienced teachers of drama. They have been writing together for more years than they wish to remember. Skidmore writes the consonants and Barlow writes the vowels. They are always arguing about punctuation. Despite this they have written many books and plays including *Paper Tigers* (OUP), *The Lost Diaries* and *The Dark Forest* series (HarperCollins), and *The Mad Myths* and *Vernon Bright* series (Puffin), as well as several books for teenagers: *I Fell in Love with a Leather Jacket*, *In Love with an Urban Gorilla* and *Dream On!* (Piccadilly Press). They have also worked as series editors for *High Impact* with Heinemann. They are well known for their appearances at literary festivals and schools up and down the country, where their presentations have been variously described as 'brilliant', 'hilarious' and 'mad'. When they are not writing, Barlow likes to go sailing and Skidmore likes to go and and watch Leicester Tigers RFC. Their answers to their most frequently asked questions are:

Yes, we have met JK Rowling;
No, we can't get you her autograph;
Yes, we will write anything for money;
No, we are not rich.

Anthony Masters

Anthony Masters began writing when he was sixteen and his work includes novels about adults and young people. He has published *Finding Joe* (Scholastic), *The Drop* (Orchard), *The Black Dogs of Doom* (Bloomsbury) and *Wicked* (Orchard and Heinemann New Windmills). His approach to a book is to write a 'splurge' – a stream of consciousness – where he is able to hold the narrative in his mind and produce solid chunks of prose that are completely unstructured. Then, rather like a sculptor, he carves the chunks into a communicating shape, and produces many drafts of the book until the final result is achieved. Anthony Masters works closely with young people in adventure workshops, creating confidence and adrenalin for writing. His workshops include 'Book Explosions' and 'Location Writing'.

George Kulbacki and Di Timmins

United by a need to write entertaining and accessible school plays, and a desire for a good laugh, George Kulbacki and Diana Timmins embarked upon collaborative writing in 1997. Together they have written two full-length plays, *Grandmother's Footsteps* and *Time Travelling for Beginners* along with many short plays for reading and performance. George was born in Preston and much to his own, and everyone else's surprise, graduated from Keele University in 1984. An occasional poet, playwright and songwriter, he unintentionally drifted into teaching, eventually arriving at Montgomery High School, Blackpool, as the Head of English in 1995. Here he met the Head of Drama and Expressive Arts, Di Timmins. Born in Blackpool, Di graduated from Bretton Hall College, Yorkshire, and, after years of producing plays, began writing when she needed something in a hurry. Di's interests include archaeology, the internet and reading. George loves all things epicurean (look it up!) and football. One day they hope to be millionaires.

Ken Campbell

Ken Campbell is well known in British theatre for his exploits as playwright, actor, director and comedian. After founding the *Ken Campbell Roadshow* (where *Home* and *Spies* originate), he set up *The Science Fiction Theatre of Liverpool*. He has directed many performances, including a record-breaking 22-hour play cycle by Neil Oram. As well as writing and directing adult plays, Ken Campbell has written plays for children (including *Old King Cole* and *Skungpoomery*), together with film and TV scripts such as *Unfair Exchanges* and *The Madness Museum*. He has also presented three science series for Channel 4: *Reality on the Rocks*, *Brainspotting* and, most recently, *Six Experiments that Changed the World*.

Mary Colson

After spending some immensely rewarding years teaching both children and adults (including a year in Prague teaching Czech air-traffic controllers English), Mary decided to leave the classroom and concentrate fully on her writing. She is currently on the MA course in Creative Writing at the University of East Anglia, specialising in scriptwriting. Her main writing interest is playwriting, and she has recently completed *Bloodwater*, a family drama centred around memory and perceptions of the past. She is currently working on her first full-length filmscript, *Safe*, a modern-day western set in the final urban frontier, Milton Keynes. In her spare time Mary is a keen musician, playing the French horn with various groups, and she is a proud aunt to Daniel, Alex and Corrie and a godmother to Megan. Creative stimulus is her reason for travelling widely – she says – this is a lie but she has some nice photos and some intriguing stamps in her passport. Mary is hoping to persuade someone to sponsor her next project, which will require a lengthy period of research in South America . . .

Ann Cartwright

Ann Cartwright is an English and Drama teacher from the West Midlands. She lives in Walsall. As a child, she was always interested in reading, writing and drama, taking part in assemblies and plays at school. Her greatest interest was the cinema. She was fascinated with dialogue, its immediate power and meaning conveyed without paragraphed narrative. She took an honours degree in English and somehow stumbled into primary teaching. Through fate and job vacancies, she found herself in secondary teaching and drama. Because she needed resources, she began to write her own scripts and school productions, including the text and librettos for musicals. Eventually, she sent off some of her resources to Heinemann, and these were successfully published as *Forty Short Plays* in 2000. She is a Christian and still enjoys cinema, music, writing and gardening. Her next target is to write a children's novel.

David Calcutt

David has written ever since he can remember, but first became interested in playwriting when he was at college, where he wrote short sketches for the Poetry and Drama Society. Later, when he was a teacher, he wrote plays for his students, and after he left teaching he wrote for a youth theatre he was running, and his own small-scale touring company. His work has always been very practical because of this – he has always made sure that what he writes can be performed. It's a good discipline for a playwright. And now, even if he's not writing for a particular group or company, he still creates an imaginary one, just to make sure the thing works. He's written quite a few plays for young people and schools. Several of these have been published, including *Tess of the d'Urbervilles*, *Dracula*, *The Labyrinth: The story of Theseus and the Minotaur* (Oxford University Press: Playscripts), *The Terrible Fate of Humpty Dumpty*, *Treasure Island*, *Homer's Odyssey*, *Dr Jekyll and Mr Hyde*, *Gawain and the Green Knight*, *The Island of Doctor Moreau* (NelsonThornes: Dramascripts), *Detention*

(Heinemann), *Gifts of Flame* (Faber and Faber). His most recently produced play for young people is *Tongues of Flame*, which was written for Woldingham Girls School. Also, for radio, he has written four-part adaptations of two of Susan Cooper's novels from 'The Dark Is Rising' sequence.

Chris Burgess

Chris Burgess has had experience in amateur dramatics since his own schooldays. He began writing plays soon after beginning a teaching career in English and Drama. His first book, *Short Plays for Large Classes*, is designed to provide speaking parts for every pupil in a class. He has written and produced numerous plays for secondary schools, including *By Sword and Spell*, a full-length play about the boyhood of King Arthur. One-act plays include *A Stranger in No-man's Land*, *A Letter of Marque*, *Frontier Incident* and *Little Tomboy*. His experience includes writing and presenting scripts for BBC Schools Radio and acting in productions at the Keighley Playhouse in West Yorkshire. He has also written English Language books for schools, including *Discovering the Theatre*.